THE LAST DAYS OF STEAM AROUND

LONDON

THE LAST DAYS OF STEAM AROUND
LONDON

KEVIN ROBERTSON

ALAN SUTTON
1988

ALAN SUTTON PUBLISHING
BRUNSWICK ROAD · GLOUCESTER

First published 1988

British Library Cataloguing in Publication Data

Robertson, Kevin
Last days of steam around London.
1. South-east England. Railway services, 1935–1947
I. Title
385′.09422

ISBN 0-86299-502-7

*Endpapers: Front, Paddington, the only London terminus
of the Great Western – M. Mensing
Back, No. 60056 'Centenary' rests at Kings Cross – M. Mensing*

*Front Cover: No. 46240, 'City of Coventry' at
Camden shed – Barry Eagles
No. 60130 'Kestral' at Kings Cross – Colour Rail
No. 6015 'King Richard III' near Seer Green with
the Birmingham–Paddington express – Colour Rail
No. 34101 'Hartland' on the 'Golden
Arrow' Service, seen here leaving Victoria on 1.4.60 – Colour Rail*

Typesetting and origination by
Alan Sutton Publishing Limited
Printed in Great Britain by
Dotesios Printers Limited

For Hugh Abbinnett — a railwayman and an enthusiast

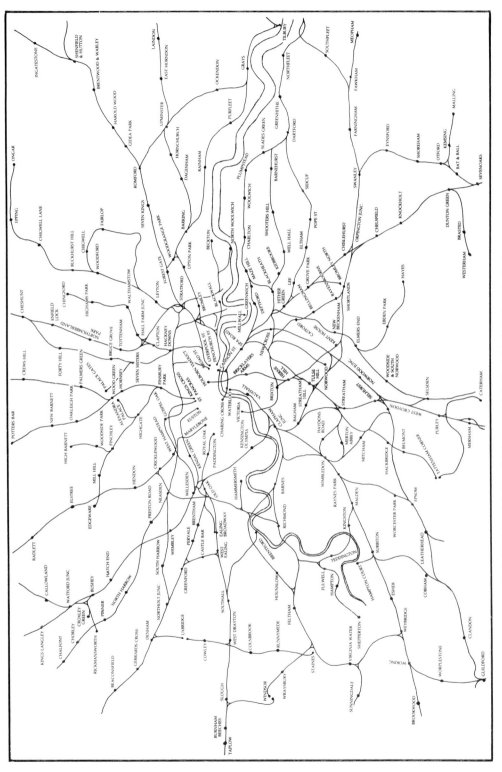

LAST DAYS OF STEAM AROUND LONDON

Only principal railways and stations are shown

Introduction

The immediate reaction when thinking of London would probably be the tourist sites; perhaps Buckingham Palace or the Houses of Parliament – depending of course on one's personal viewpoint.

However, London to the steam railway enthusiast was a mecca without equal anywhere in the country. Here at various terminals engines, large and small, representing all four pre-nationalisation companies could be seen. Most were on express passenger workings, but in the background smaller machines could be seen fussing to and fro, shunting the stock ready for the next working.

Unfortunately, I like many others spent most of my time at just one station and I could now kick myself for not having savoured the delights of other locations. Consequently, when asked to produce this the latest volume in the series, it came as an opportunity to rectify the omission of years past and provide a wider glimpse of steam workings from 1948 to their demise.

More than any other area, however, London is extremely difficult to portray in a single volume; especially when one is restricted to a limited number of pages for a book. Accordingly, I have attempted to portray both locations and engines across a broad spectrum and I apologise in advance if a particular favourite is missing.

I do hope the final result will have an appeal, if it brings back a few memories then all will have been worthwhile.

I would like to record my thanks to all those photographers whose work appears in the book. In addition thanks are due to a number of the 'back room staff', for without their help none of this would have been possible. Hugh Abbinnett, David Abbott, John Fry, Reg Randell, Dennis Tillman, Ron White and Ian Shawyer. And of course Lyn – what would I do without her?

Kevin Robertson

THE LAST DAYS OF STEAM AROUND
LONDON

The Western Region

At first glance the task of briefly describing the Western Region and its environs around London would appear to be an easy one as there is but one terminus involved, Paddington. Here under a cavernous roof, in some ways more akin to a cathedral than a railway station, Brunel terminated his main line from Bristol, which later became part of the famous Great Western Railway. Standing alongside Paddington the 'Great Western Royal Hotel' is a superb building of grandiose proportions and very much in keeping with the station itself.

The start of countless journeys at the Paddington booking office. Here one could buy a ticket to almost any destination in the country – as well as a considerable number abroad. The clerks were well experienced in knowing both the location of the actual ticket required as well as its price, in *£. s. d.* of course!

British Railways

Nowadays it is easy to dismiss the heady excitement of those days 150 years ago, when the first trains on the embryo GWR commenced running from London to Maidenhead and later Bristol. Indeed originally the GWR had intended turning north to link with the London & Birmingham line to Euston and so operating a joint terminus. Practicalities, however, forced a change of heart, the most obvious of which was that the L & B used 'narrow gauge' whilst the GWR had adopted Brunel's 'broad gauge'.

So it was that after a brief time spent at a temporary terminus west of Paddington the line was finally extended to the site of the present station although, this was not to be the final limit of GWR influence as later running powers were extended to parts of the Metropolitan Railway, a broad gauge line which was steam-hauled when it first opened.

The strength of the GWR lay in the fact that there was never any real threat to its monopoly of traffic on its lines into London. Consequently at the time of 'the grouping' the GWR was unique in that it retained not only its name, but also absorbed into the fold a number of smaller concerns. Most of these absorbed lines were situated in South Wales and so are out of the scope of this brief monologue.

Despite the earlier failed attempt at a connection with the L & B line, the GWR did make connections with a number of other lines within the London area. Among these was the line from Old Oak, northwest through High Wycombe, which became part of the main line from Paddington to Birmingham avoiding the congestion around Reading and Oxford. In the case of the High Wycombe route the joint parties involved were the Great Central and its successor the London and North Eastern Railway. Joint arrangements also existed with the LMS on the West London Extension line and at one time running powers over the LBSCR to Victoria via the aforementioned West London line through Clapham Junction.

This link to Victoria is especially interesting, as for a while there was a slip coach service on London bound trains which was detached at Ealing and then hauled over the LBSCR line to their terminus. From 1910 in order to combat a rival LNWR through service from the Midlands to Broad Street station they started another through service to Wolverhampton from Victoria, although this did not last long. The GWR were eventually content to surrender all rights of access to the Southern station coinciding with 'the grouping' of 1923.

The main GWR locomotive depôt at London was at the delightfully named Old Oak, although, as with the LSWR depôt at Nine Elms, one can only ponder on the original reason for such names. In addition to the locomotive shed, a vast array of sidings were arranged on an adjacent site with the connection to the West London line opposite. Another part of this passed over the main GWR route to connect a little further north with the marshalling yards of Willesden on the LMS line. As such one can gauge the proximity of the LMS and GWR routes and so see the reason for the original interest in taking the GWR route northwards into Euston.

The locomotive depôt at Old Oak had itself replaced an earlier, smaller depôt at Westbourne Park, although this did have the advantage of being nearer to the terminus. As a result of moving the servicing facilities further out a small stabling yard was established at Ranelagh Bridge near Royal Oak. This was used by locomotives requiring just minor servicing, turning facilities were also provided here. Ranelagh Bridge continued in use as a stabling point for diesel traction long after the demise of steam working, finally becoming redundant with the introduction of the HST sets. Not far from Old Oak and within earshot of the main line is HM Prison at Wormwood Scrubs, from where the master spy George Blake escaped in October 1966.

2

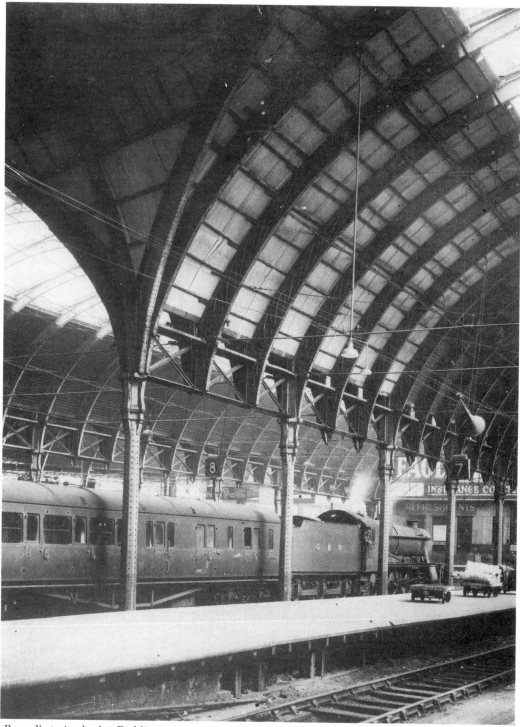

Brunel's train shed at Paddington in 1946. The photograph was taken to show the new covering to Platforms 7 & 8, damaged earlier in an air-raid. The engine is No. 1002 which was later named *County of Berks*.

British Railways

Adjacent to the passenger terminus at Paddington was the GWR goods depôt, rail access to this was available from the relief lines leading into the passenger station. Between the passenger and goods stations the Metropolitan railway ran from Hammersmith and passed under the main lines by Westbourne Park (Metropolitan) station. In this way there was no disruption to traffic on any of the routes mentioned.

As well as its passenger workings, the GWR had a considerable number of yards, goods depôts and docks around the capital. One of these, South Lambeth, was in fact deep in what could really be described as SR territory, although it remained an oasis of GWR influence right up to the time of nationalisation.

Another less well known fact is that the GWR operated an electric service on the Ealing to Shepherds Bush line. This was later absorbed into the London Underground network and now forms part of the present day Central Line.

Moving west away from London there was little in the way of commuter traffic compared with the other companies. However, some commuter traffic emerged as places like Hayes, Langley, Burnham and Maidenhead became increasingly popular as desirable places to live. A similar situation occurred on the line through Gerrards Cross to High Wycombe, which was developed using the theme of 'Living in Metroland'.

Consequently, this reduced peak hour traffic makes it appropriate to refer to the GWR's various minor lines in the London area as branches. Indeed, branch lines they

Bank holiday crowds on 'The Lawn' at Paddington, Saturday 31.7.43. Despite the fact that this was wartime the number of passengers wishing to get away for a break was considerable and added to the pressure already existing on the network due to the movement of munitions and troops in connection with the war effort.

British Railways

4

were in every sense of the word; West Drayton to Staines, Slough to Windsor, West Drayton to Uxbridge, all three connecting with the main line itself. Two of these were also served by other routes, Windsor by the LSWR from Staines whilst Uxbridge also had a line reaching it from Denham. However, no physical connections existed between the various terminals even if in the same towns. Later on as a result of an increase in residential development it became appropriate to refer to the branches from Maidenhead to Marlow and also Loudwater as coming within the London area. The reference to the Windsor branch is of particular interest, as it is here that the railway passes close to Eton college which had fought the intrusion of the railway with every means at its disposal back in the 1830s.

Unlike the SR the GWR never developed electirification as a means of propulsion on the main line, although this was certainly investigated from time to time. Instead steam remained supreme well into BR days although its use from 1958 onwards declined steadily. Gradually, however, the main line and suburban services succumbed to the diesels, with the final steam working out of Paddington in late 1965. As to the future, who knows, for in connection with the recent rebuilding of the Lawn (the popular name given to the station's circulation concourse), the opportunity was taken to erect end posts suitable for use with overhead wires. Indeed there has even been talk recently as to a new link from Paddington to Heathrow which would be electrified from the start. We may yet see electric services out of Paddington, where for so long the 'Castles' and 'Kings' reigned supreme.

LONDON

IT'S QUICKER BY RAIL

Shrewsbury

Birmingham

Hereford

South Wales Worcester

Bristol Oxford

PADDINGTON

Exeter

Penzance

Plymouth

Paddington, the sole London terminus of that most famous of all lines, the Great Western. Seen here in 1961 with No. 5025, *Chirk Castle* after arrival on the 6.45 a.m. express from Wolverhampton Low Level.

M. Mensing

Late afternoon at Paddington, where from a vantage point at the west end of the station three steam-hauled expresses can be seen. From left to right they are No. 5034 *Corfe Castle*, No. 6867 *Peterston Grange* (on the 4.35 p.m. Paddington–Cheltenham express) and No. 1005 *County of Devon*, none of which survived into preservation.

British Railways

Some of the last duties performed by the 'Kings' were on the Newbury Race trains in 1962. No. 6012 *King Edward VI* awaiting departure from Paddington for Newbury with a special working in August 1962.

Roger Sherlock

The crew of No. 6000 *King George V* posed for the camera prior to working the 'Royal Duchy' express to the west. The bell on the framing was presented to the engine to commemorate its visit to America in 1927. In recent years controversy has surrounded the bell, is it in fact the original article? The 'King' worked the train as far as Plymouth where a change was made to a smaller, lighter engine for the trip across the Royal Albert bridge into Cornwall.

'R.A.' Collection

A brand new BR Mk. 1 coach is included here in the formation of the 'Royal Duchy' on 28.1.57. This was probably part of the train attached to the engine seen in the previous view. In the background an ex-GWR vehicle is coupled next to the Mk. 1.

'R.A.' Collection

9

The Worcester-based 'Castle' No. 7013 *Bristol Castle* awaiting departure from Platform 1 at Paddington with the 1.30 p.m. express for Paignton. This was one of the last batch of the class to be built in 1948, being withdrawn just 17 years later. (In 1952 this engine swapped identities with No. 4082 *Windsor Castle* and was then used to haul the funeral train of King George VI.)

'R.A.' Collection

Ready for the off! No. 6016 *King Edward V* at the head of the 6.08 p.m. from Paddington to
Shrewsbury on 8.6.62. Records show that on this particular day the service was extended to
Wrexham, although how often this took place is not clear.

M. Mensing

With 14 minutes still to go before departure, No. 6013 *King Henry VIII* draws admiring glances
from some passengers whilst waiting to leave on the 1.30 p.m. to Penzance. Alongside is No. 5946
Marwell Hall on the 1.20 p.m. to Weymouth (via Newbury and Castle Cary). At the time both
Paddington and Waterloo vied with each other for services to the Dorset port. The squat boiler of
the 'King' shows up well against that of the smaller 'Hall' class engine. 13.4.58.

M. Mensing

11

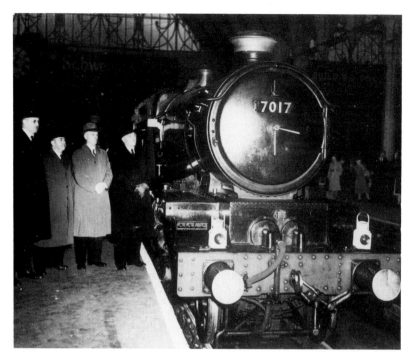

A momentus occasion at Paddington, 29.10.48 with the naming of a brand new 'Castle', No. 7017 *G.J. Churchward* in honour of the locomotive designer. The ceremony was performed by Capt. W. Gregson, RNR, the engine is seen with the curtains still draped near the new nameplate.
'R.A.' Collection

Another naming ceremony, this time No. 7001 *Sir James Milne*. Sir James is seen alongside his namesake at Paddington, 23.4.48; he was the last General Manager of the independent GWR company, but was so anti-nationalisation that he refused the offer of the chairmanship of the newly formed railway executive. Summing up this attitude to the writer more that 30 years later at Shrewsbury, an old Great Western man remarked, ' . . . the only thing wrong the nationalisation was that it wasn't the 'Western that nationalised the others . . . !'
'R.A.' Collection

At the same time as the LMS were developing their own diesel locomotives, the GWR placed an order for a gas turbine machine from the Swiss manufacturer Brown-Boveri. At 2,500 hp it was considerably more powerful than anything else around at the time. Unfortunately, delays in construction meant that delivery was not until a year after nationalisation. The engine is seen here at Paddington arousing a considerable amount of interest. Besides the engine, note the longitudinal baulks on which the track is laid, similar to that used on the GWR over a century beforehand.

'R.A.' Collection

Another 'Castle' class engine to carry the name of a famous personage associated with the GWR was No. 5069 *Isambard Kingdom Brunel*, the nameplate for which had to be specially made to accommodate the 21 letters involved. Depending on your affinity, or otherwise, to the 'Western the 'Castles' were either loved or hated. However, it must be admitted that their performance was usually totally out of proportion to their relatively small size. They performed prodigious feats hauling trains that were often far heavier than those pulled by today's much more powerful diesels. Notice too the old pattern electric ground signal in the foreground.

Roger Sherlock

Several members of the 'Britannia' class were allocated to the Western Region, with the majority concentrated on either Hereford or Cardiff (Canton) sheds. Here No. 70023 *Venus* blows off impatiently from the safety valves at the head of the 'Capitals United Express'.

Roger Sherlock

As well as passengers Paddington also dealt with a vast amount of parcels and other freight, although it must be said that milk churns were something of a rarity at the terminus itself. The three men are engaged in the labour intensive activity of unloading a British Railways road vehicle supposedly as late as 1962.

'R.A.' Collection

Moving smartly backwards out of the station is No. 6002 *King William IV* after arriving with a train from Birkenhead in 1950. In the background is the roof of the extensive Paddington goods depôt which was very near the passenger station. At the time of writing the goods depôt is now just a barren wasteland, although proposals to redevelop this former railway site have been mooted.

W. Gilburt

No. 6959 *Peating Hall* arriving at the terminus with an up express. The engine is attached to one of the later design flat-sided tenders, with at least part of the train formed of modern BR Mk. 1 rolling stock. In the background an underground train on a Metropolitan line service can be seen.

Roger Sherlock

A pair of the short-lived 'Blue Pullman' trains arriving at Paddington, probably around 1962. In many respects these units were the forerunners of today's HST sets, although they differed in that the accommodation was intended as one class only. Also in the event of a power-car failure substitution of the locomotive section was a far more involved procedure. From Paddington the trains operated to Bristol and Birmingham (the latter service also ran from Marylebone for a while) and consisted of an eight coach formation.

British Railways

Unusual motive power for station pilot duties at Paddington. This was normally performed by a pannier tank, but here No. 4915 *Condover Hall* is making hard work of drawing out the empty stock of an up service from Wolverhampton on 21.10.61.

M. Mensing

Viewed from the west end of Platform 1, No. 5917 *Westminster Hall* backs out of Paddington with the empty stock of the 9.17 a.m. service for Great Malvern on Sunday 13.4.58. Out of sight at the other end of the train was a 94xx pannier tank No. 9422, which judging from the lack of visible exhaust from No. 5917 was doing all the work!

M. Mensing

A breather for the fireman, as No. 70026 *Polar Star* brings the up 'Red Dragon' service the final few yards into Paddington on its journey from Cardiff. This was the engine which was later involved in the Milton accident of 1955, which is described in detail in the companion volume *The Last Days of Steam in Berkshire*.

'R.A.' Collection

18

An impressive low angle view of the gas turbine engine, No.18000 seen here just outside Paddington in May 1950. Despite its modern interior a careful look at the cab roof reveals a steam engine-type whistle, the power being provided by a compressed air supply.

'R.A.' Collection

A second gas turbine engine was ordered from the British firm of Metropolitan-Vickers and was delivered for service in December 1951. Like its earlier sister it was never officially named although both were sometimes referred to as 'Kerosene Castle' a comment on the smell which both engines emitted. After some years in service No. 18100 was later stripped internally and converted to overhead electric working for use on the 25 kV a.c. line out of Euston.

British Railways

Largest of the diesel-hydraulic types introduced on the WR were the appropriately named 'Western' diesels. No. D1005 *Western Venturer* near Ranelagh Bridge in 1963. In many people's opinion these were amongst the best looking of all diesel types, although some drivers said that the engines often developed a peculiar oscillation that could cause what amounted to motion sickness.

British Railways

The GWR had pioneered the use of diesel cars as early as 1934 which were used on many parts of the system. This is one of the special parcel vehicles entering Paddington in 1950, still resplendent in its GWR livery.

W. Gilburt

A number of engines were converted by the GWR to oil-burning during a brief episode from 1946 onwards. However, photographs of them on trains are rare. Here though No. 5955 *Garth Hall* is at the head of a westbound express leaving Paddington in 1946. (The engine was later re-numbered 3955 for the remainder of its time as an oil-burner.)

W. Gilburt

On its return journey to Wales, the driver of No. 70023 *Venus* opens up his engine as he passes the Paddington newspaper platform with the down 'Capitals United Express' in March 1957.

W. Gilburt

Moving away from trains for a moment into the quiet of the classroom at the Signal School at Royal Oak instead. This was where men and youths intent on becoming signalmen attended a series of lectures before being tested on their competence. The system had changed little over the years, this 1961 view showing the same type of signal instruments that had been in use for decades. In the background is an extensive model railway, which was fully signalled and used for demonstration purposes. Much of the equipment from this was later thrown away as scrap.

British Railways

A parcels working at Westbourne Park on a murky October day. An unidentified 49xx 'Hall' at the head of just four vans most of which appear to be of ex-LMS origin.

W. Gilburt

A suburban steam service at Westbourne Park during 1950. 'Big Prairie' No. 6169 is at the head of some elderly bogie stock which is dwarfed by the bulk of the engine. The 61xx series of engines were popular for this type of duty as they were powerful machines capable of a good turn of speed when required.

W. Gilburt

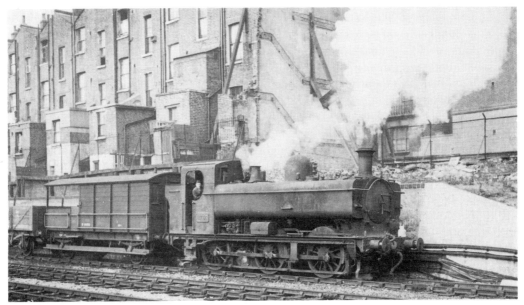

No series of photographs of any area in the Western Region would be complete without a view of a pannier tank. No. 8757, one of the later series of 57xx machines, shunting near to Westbourne Park in November 1949.

W. Gilburt

Shrewsbury allocated 'Castle', No. 7015 *Carn Brea Castle* at rest at Old Oak Common depôt, 23.9.62. This was one of the last in this series of the class, although it is shown here attached to an older style tender. Compared with the earlier batch of machines No. 7015 had been fitted with higher degree superheat and double chimney, the latter still retaining its copper band in distinctive 'Western style. The front covers to the centre cylinder valve guides were also a slightly different shape from earlier engines.

Roger Sherlock

24

King George V again at rest at Old Oak in August 1954. In the following year the complete class of 30 'King' engines were withdrawn from service following a fatigue failure on one of the front bogies. Fortunately matters were soon put right and the class remained in service until the end of 1962. No. 6000 is now preserved in running order as part of the National Collection.

W. Gilburt

The 15xx series of pannier tank were primarily used for shunting within the London area, their short wheelbase making them ideal for working in confined locations even if at speed the ride tended to be rough. This is No. 1503, one of a class of only ten engines introduced as recently as 1949. They were in effect the final derivative of the standard pannier tank, incorporating outside cylinders and valve gear allied to a standard boiler. No. 1503 is seen at Old Oak, a lot of their time being spent on moving empty coaching stock to and from Paddington.

W. Gilburt

25

A rarely photographed engine was No. 4900 *Saint Martin* which started life as a 'Saint' class 4-6-0 before being modified as the prototype for the numerous and successful 'Hall' class. No. 4900 is alongside the carriage shed at Old Oak in early BR days.

Roger Sherlock

Taken at the same location as the previous view, this photograph is of No. 1025 *County of Radnor* in what appears to be overall black livery with a red background to the name and number plates. Also the engine is in its original condition without a double chimney, the class being the only 'Western engines in later years to adopt a straight nameplate, although still in the basic Swindon style.

Roger Sherlock

One of Old Oak's allocation of 61xx tanks, No. 6143 alongside the coaling stage at its home depôt in August 1963. By this time much of the work formerly undertaken by these engines had been turned over to diesel units, with the class filling in time on freight turns or perhaps covering for a failed diesel until the moment came for withdrawal.

M.N.L.P.S.

An early series 'Castle' this time, No. 4078 *Pembroke Castle* in a nice clean condition at Old Oak during the summer of 1954. This was a Landore-based engine, a shed which had a reputation for cleanliness almost to the very end of main line steam working.

W. Gilburt

Final days at Old Oak, and perhaps the last two steam engines to leave the depôt on 21.3.65. The two crews are posed for the camera with the loco inspector in the centre.

'R.A.' Collection

No. 7025 *Sudeley Castle* at its home depôt of Old Oak in 1954. At the time No. 7025 was only five years old but was covered in an all pervading layer of grime. In an active life of just fifteen years the engine ran an estimated 700,000 miles.

W. Gilburt

West Ealing mechanical signalbox in 1955. It was eventually rendered redundant in 1968 by the WR panel box at O.O.C. This particular signalbox was originally built as an all timber structure, but a brick lower skin was added at a later date. Notice also the long brick building adjoining the 'box which acted as a relay room.

British Railways

Searchlight signals, the predecessors to today's M.A.S. heads on the WR main line near Ealing. The long shield was intended to reduce the glare from above so as not to be seen from aircraft. Notice also how the signal post and other fittings are still of the standard heavy type associated with mechanical action – streamlined posts were still some years away. In the background is a 97xx condensing series pannier tank which was fitted in this way so as to be able to work over parts of the underground Metropolitan line.

British Railways

Moving on we come to Southall, pronounced 'Sarf'all' by some of the porters. No. 6133 is on the up local line at the head of a six coach rake, whilst another 97xx series condensing pannier is just visible in the bay. To the left are the up and down main lines which can be clearly seen to follow a straighter path through the station thus allowing for faster speeds.

M.N.L.P.S.

The GWR 2-6-0 'Mogul' design dated back to 1911 although a number survived in service right up to the very end of steam. This is No. 5333 of the second batch of engines to be built and seen outside Southall shed in 1958. Alongside is one of the original Western diesel railcars.

M.N.L.P.S.

No. 5933 formerly *Kingsway Hall* at Southall in April 1965. At this time steam had only a matter of months left to survive on the Western Region and this can perhaps be appreciated from the run down appearance of the engine.

Roger Sherlock

Servicing No. 5933 at Southall, the pile of discarded fire irons and other steam engine memorabilia in the foreground a gaunt reminder of locomotives gone before.

Roger Sherlock

By April 1965 there was just one 'Castle' left in active service, No. 7029 *Clun Castle* seen here under the sheer legs at Southall, bereft of name and cabside number plates. To this engine would come the melancholy task of working the last steam train out of Paddington some months later in November 1965. The engine is now preserved and aside from being a regular performer on a number of steam specials it can often be seen at its home base of Tyseley.

Roger Sherlock

An essential but rarely photographed aspect of railway maintainance, weedkilling, seen from the trackside near West Drayton in 1953. The WR operated two weedkilling trains, principally during the early spring and early autumn, with the intention of checking the growth of weeds which might otherwise slow drainage through the ballast and so eventually affect track alignment.

British Railways

One of the delightful 14xx 0-4-2Ts, posed on the turntable at Slough in April 1962. No. 1421 was a regular performer on the WR Windsor branch until ousted by diesel traction.

British Railways

Permanent way work was reckoned to be one of the hardest manual tasks on the railway because of the amount of bending involved. This is Ganger Seller of Gang No. 29, Maidenhead in the process of replacing an oak key into the rail chair during the daily inspection of his length.

British Railways

Guard Gillcrest sorting newspapers ready for delivery at Ealing in 1962. This task was regularly performed by the guard, but it was often not appreciated that he had to have each bundle ready in advance of the station stop to avoid delaying his service.

Collection of P.T. Earl

Moving away from Paddington now and this time to Marylebone (Marylebone is referred to again in the Eastern Region section). At the platform is No. 6129 with the headcode to work a stopping passenger service up the joint line towards High Wycombe. Stopping services on this route commenced from both Marylebone and Paddington.

W. Gilburt

Again on the joint line, this is Beaconsfield but with an ex-LNER 'L1' tank, No. 67767 on a stopping service.

W. Gilburt

On a hot summer day in 1954, No. 6964 *Thornbridge Hall* disturbs the peace of Beaconsfield with a five-coach non-stop service, carrying a Class 'A' or express passenger headcode. Along with several of the stations on this particular line, the platforms were built alongside loops on either side of the main line with the intention of providing a refuge for slower services which might otherwise impede the crack Birmingham 2-hour expresses.

W. Gilburt

Northwest to High Wycombe and another 'L1', this time No. 67798 on a stopping service, 14.8.58. High Wycombe was also the junction station for the Western branch line through Loudwater and Wooburn Green to Bourne End and Marlow and was worked by tank engines from Maidenhead shed.

W. Gilburt

Inside Latchmere Junction signalbox on the WLER line with Signalman C.H. Bailey on duty. This was a 'Western 'box but with connections onto the nearby Southern route – hence the reason for the SR instrument on the left-hand side of the blockshelf. The whole interior is clean, polished and a credit to the regular men. Notice the black and white levers which are for placing detonators on the track in case of emergency.

'R.A.' Collection

A considerable amount of parcels traffic was dealt with at Kensington (Olympia). No. 5993 *Kirby Hall* seen at the head of the Kensington–West of England via Bristol parcels service in March 1961.
Photomatic

A close up of No. 9700 at Addison Road, 24.3.57. In steam days it was common practice to maintain a tank engine at this location for shunting purposes. No. 9700 attached to a motley selection of vehicles all of which, with the exception of the first, appear to be of GWR origin.
Derek Clayton

Filming at Olympia in June 1966. The occasion was a visit of the *Blue Peter* presenters Christopher Trace and John Noakes to the Motorail terminal. Of course John Noakes has 'Patch' in attendance.
British Railways

District line underground stock on the Earls Court–Olympia service in 1957, the BR tracks of the former West London extension railway are on the right.

Derek Clayton

The final regular workings of steam in London involved a number of ex-GWR pannier tanks sold out of service by the Western Region to London Transport. This is No. L99 shunting at Neasden in 1968 with the chimney of the former power station in the background. Few people knew of the existence of these engines at the time as they were employed on engineering services around the Neasden area. A delightful letter appeared in *The Times* about this period in which the sender wrote, ' . . . I was awoken the other morning by what I took to be a steam engine passing under my window. Being under the impression that such old-fashioned machines had been banished many years past I had to get up to check if my hearing was right. Where was the thing going, and do British Railways know anything about it?' They were truly the last regular steam engines working in London.

'R.A.' Collection

The Southern Region

At the time of nationalisation the Southern was unique among the railways of Britain in that it possessed the highest proportion of electrified line. They also had the potential to increase this percentage as and when time and funds permitted.

How such a progressive attitude came about can be traced back to the days of Edwardian splendour when the London, Brighton & South Coast Railway electrified its South London line from Victoria to London Bridge. They used overhead wires, rather than a third rail, similar to that seen today at Euston and Kings Cross.

As with the LMS and LNER groups, the Southern Railway company had been formed in 1923 and was made up of three main constituents. The principal company was, without doubt, the London & South Western whose main lines stretched west from Waterloo to Bournemouth, Exeter and beyond, as well as a multitude of suburban routes. Many of the latter were themselves instrumental in the development of much of Surrey as a desirable place to live.

The approach to the LSWR terminus at Waterloo not long after the rebuilding 1892. These were the days of excellence in mechanical signalling, with the driver being expected to know which signal applied to his particular route. To the extreme right was the little necropolis station from which regular funeral trains ran to the cemetery at Brookwood.

Lens of Sutton

43

A period scene of the circulating area at Waterloo LSWR.

Collection of Reg Randell

It was probably as much to do with route mileage as anything else that enabled the LSWR to take the leading role in the newly formed Southern group. The former general manager of the LSWR, Sir Herbert Walker took over the same role as head of the new organisation. Accordingly, LSWR influence concerning electrification came to the fore, as less than six years later the South London line was electrified, the third rail network was started, which from the outset proved to be such a success on both suburban and main line workings.

Therefore, when the time came to expand the electrified network it was the third rail system that was chosen. Today that same system stretches west to Bournemouth and Weymouth, as well as covering almost every passenger worked line in Kent, Sussex and Surrey.

East of the former LSWR lines were those routes previously operated by the LBSCR. The principal line being the Brighton route from Victoria. To try and do justice to such an undertaking as the LBSCR in a few short lines is verging on the impossible, but suffice it to say that this company also operated a network of suburban lines (the term branch line is singularly out of place on the LBSCR), principally in south London. In some places the LSWR and LBSCR also came into contact, although perhaps the word conflict seemed to be more appropriate. Clapham Junction and Portsmouth are the two which readily spring to mind, but countless others could well be mentioned. This resulted from each company either having duplicate lines to serve the same location or by being forced to accept a compromise whereby a sharing of traffic existed. To the directors such a move may well have been the only feasible, if reluctantly acceptable, solution although to the men on the ground charged with the administration of such an arrangement there

44

was inevitably an atmosphere of mistrust. Unfortunately, old habits die hard and consequently in 1923 with both concerns now theoretically on the same side, it was still some time before harmony reigned.

Another example of those extraordinary days, when politics took precedence over practicalities, is in the number of dupiicated routes. Witness, even today the number of ways it is still possible to travel to places like Sutton or Croyden. The changing architecture of adjacent stations is yet another clue to the differences of decades past.

The third company to be incorporated into the Southern was the South Eastern and Chatham Railway, itself an earlier amalgamation of the South Eastern and London Chatham & Dover Companies. Besides operating its own London stations at Holborn Viaduct, Charing Cross, Cannon Street, London Bridge and Blackfriars (St Pauls), the SECR operated alongside the LBSCR at Victoria and London Bridge, giving rise to references to the 'Brighton' and 'Eastern' sides of the station. Indeed it is still referred to as such today, and it is easy to see from the physical appearance of Victoria that it had formally been two stations side by side. Similarly, London Bridge was, and still is, referred to as having a 'South Eastern' and a 'Brighton' side, with platforms 7 and 8 on the former SECR terminal lines. These had themselves been part of the original London and Greenwich railway and it was because the L&G was charging the SECR and LBSCR so much for the use of the site that a new station had been built at Bricklayers Arms.

To add still further to the confusion, the SECR also had a station called Waterloo, this was not far from the LSWR terminus between which a rail connection existed until the First World War. British Rail in an attempt to prevent undue passenger confusion use letters to differentiate between the platforms at Waterloo East with conventional numbers being used at the terminus. Even so, with both stations a matter of yards apart mistakes by unwary passengers are not altogether unknown.

Steam express at the turn of the century, Adams 'T3' 4-4-0, No. 570 at Woking on a Waterloo–Exeter working.

Lens of Sutton

Like the other concerns already mentioned, the SECR operated suburban services which stretched out into north Kent, as well coming into conflict (or competition depending on one's viewpoint) with the other companies at Guildford and as far out as Reading – Guildford was the only station which prior to 1923 regularly dealt with trains from all three pre-group railways. While the LSWR may have had Hampshire and the West Country – the latter fought over with the GWR – and the LBSCR much of Sussex, the SECR had a monopoly of the Kent ports at Dover and Folkestone, hence its prestigious routes were those on which the boat trains operated from Victoria and Charing Cross.

Additional boat trains operated from the other SR London stations, including trains to Southampton from Waterloo and Victoria to Newhaven. But it was the boat trains to the Kent channel ports that were the most numerous, the best known being the 'Golden Arrow' from Victoria to Dover.

The Southern Railway inherited all of this within an area stretching from Ramsgate in the east to Padstow in the west as well as the cross-channel ferry services and lines in the Isle of Wight.

By 1925 the system had settled down under its corporate management, expansion of the third rail network was also well under way. Thus on the basis of pure economics it was the overhead network that was abandoned with all future electrification schemes for the SR using the third rail system.

Gradually electrification further expanded so that by 1948 it was principally the long distance services that remained steam-hauled, although as ever there were exceptions, with a number of local trains remaining steam-operated almost to the end. The peak hour shuttle from Clapham Junction to Kensington Olympia is just one example.

Meanwhile on the former SECR lines steam was finally ousted with the implementation of the Kent Coast electrification schemes of the late 1950s. One of the last workings from Victoria was the Oxted line, a steam service sandwiched between electric workings, which called for prompt workings by its crew – all the more difficult as locomotives became ever more run down through lack of maintainance.

Waterloo fared better, for although there had been a gradual run down of steam power from about 1960 onwards, coinciding with the previous BR announcement of a general modernisation plan, no firm decision had been reached on future traction for the Bournemouth route. Eventually, in 1964 the choice was made and from July 1967 full electrified services swished their way out of the terminus – steam had finally been banished from the SR. Diesel traction had in the meantime taken over the Exeter route.

An aside to this, forgotten by many, was the closure of many of the former steam depôts operated by the SR within London. Nine Elms on the approach to Waterloo was converted to form the new Covent Garden market although its former neighbour at Stewarts Lane remains as a servicing and maintainance point for the more modern traction. Steam on the SR may be long vanished, but its memory still lingers on.

Visit **LONDON**

TRAVEL BY TRAIN

BRITISH RAILWAYS

Salisbury — WATERLOO

Exeter — Bournemouth

Weymouth

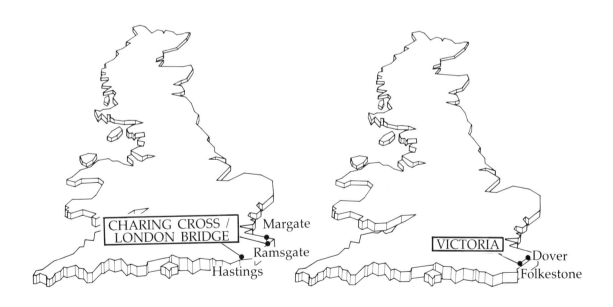

CHARING CROSS /
LONDON BRIDGE — Margate

Ramsgate

Hastings

VICTORIA — Dover

Folkestone

Synonymous with Waterloo and the steam workings throughout the 1950s were the Bulleid Pacifics. No. 35017 *Belgium Marine* seen head on with the 'Bournemouth Belle' headboard. The engine is shown in its original form before rebuilding and has probably just arrived from Nine Elms shed as there is only a single tail lamp visible.

Cedric Spiller

Another engine just backing on to its train is No. 34077 *603 Squadron* at Waterloo on 2.8.62. Just visible leaning out of the cab is the fireman with what appears to be a knotted handkerchief around his head – well remembered as common attire for many loco crews.

Roger Sherlock

The penultimate member of the 'Merchant Navy' class was No. 35029 *Ellerman Lines* waiting to start from the terminus with a down express. The engine can be seen to be already past the starting signal and so at departure time 'right-away' will probably be given verbally after consultation with the signalman. This particular engine was rescued from the scrap-merchants and placed on display at the National Railway Museum in sectionalised form, the intention being to show visitors the principles of how the steam locomotive functions.

Roger Sherlock

After arrival at Waterloo with the coaches drawn off, the main line engines would make their way, tender first, to Nine Elms depôt for servicing. Here No. 35029 *Ellerman Lines* (left) and No. 35013 *Blue Funnel* (right) cautiously negotiate the maze of pointwork outside the station on their way to the depôt.

Cedric Spiller

No. 35004 *Cunard White Star* at platform 11, Waterloo station in 1965. This particular engine was renowned as a 'good 'un' by the crews and yet she met a sad end some months before the end of steam working. Whilst working a down Bournemouth service she went into a slip near Farnborough with such force that the coupling rods buckled and a piece of tyre broke off from the wheel rim. An ignominious tow to Eastleigh resulted where, after examination, No. 35004 was condemned on the spot. She was cut up outside the front of Eastleigh running shed.

Cedric Spiller

Another engine now preserved is No. 34105 *Swanage*, which can be seen here operating trains on the Mid-Hants Railway from Alresford to Alton. At the time this photograph was taken in the 1950s the engine was based at Bournemouth and is complete with the original high side raves to the tender.

Roger Sherlock

For shunting trains in and out of Waterloo a variety of engines were used, although for many years it was the province of the small 'M7' class tanks. This is No. 30241 and at the time the photograph was taken in 1962, she was over sixty years old. She was withdrawn shortly afterwards.

Roger Sherlock

To replace and supplement the 'M7s' a variety of engines were used although it was not until the advent of the BR Class '3' machines that a really suitable engine became available. This is No. 82025 departing from the terminus and bound for the carriage sidings at Clapham Junction where the set would be serviced ready for its next working. The part of the building which can be seen on the right was the loco running foreman's office, who was responsible for overseeing the steam departures throughout a 24-hour period.

Collection of Ian Shawyer

With a crowd of admirers on the opposite platform, No. 35003 *Royal Mail* impatiently blows off steam at Waterloo on 15.8.65. The engine is in shocking external condition, but still retains its nameplates – these were removed as a precaution against pilfering shortly afterwards. Notice the AWS batteries on the front running plate as well as the unusual combination of one lamp and one train reporting disc.

R.A. Panting

A cleaner engine this time, No. 34031 *Torrington* of the smaller 'West Country' class, although in appearance it took an experienced eye to tell them apart from the larger 'Merchant Navy's'. No. 34031 was originally built with a streamlined casing, but this was subsequently removed by BR and a number of other modifications made in an effort to improve reliability. In the background the framework for the Shell building can be seen.

Roger Sherlock

A dismal autumn day sees five steam engines at Waterloo, although regretfully most are unidentifiable. What is noticable though are the deposits of ash, cinders, oil and general muck between the sleepers, which would occasionally catch light as a result of a hot cinder falling from the ashpan of a waiting engine.

Collection of Ian Shawyer

For a short while there were two regular Pullman trains from Waterloo, one of these, the 'Bournemouth Belle' is shown here with an original 'Merchant Navy' No. 35012 *United States Line* at its head.

Lens of Sutton

The other named Pullman service was the 'Devon Belle', although this was destined to have but a short life which was basically due to poor patronage. Here it awaits departure from Waterloo *c.* 1948, with the headcode of two discs centrally mounted on the buffer beam below the chimney. This indicated that the service was bound for the West of England line to Exeter via Salisbury.

Lens of Sutton

Waterloo, December 1966 and the last winter of steam working. 'Merchant Navy' No. 35023, now minus nameplates awaits departure with the 6.30 p.m. to Bournemouth.

Collection of A.J. Fry

Despite having a veritable army of 'Pacifics', the Southern Region operated a number of BR 'Standard' classes, the Class '5' 4-6-0s being the most numerous. This is No. 73119 *Elaine* shunting stock at Waterloo during the early 1960s.

Roger Sherlock

Two views of No. 35015 *Rotterdam Lloyd* (formerly No. 21C15 in SR days). The comparisons from before and after rebuilding are most interesting, especially as in the guise of No. 21C15 the engine retains the original cab.

Collection of A.J. Fry and Roger Sherlock

It is easy to forget that besides steam workings into Waterloo, electric multiple unit services had been present since 1915. BR also took over three electric locomotives to the basic SR design, although they were rare visitors to Waterloo, spending most of their time on the Central and Eastern sections of the region. The appearance of No. 20003 at Waterloo on 22.3.50 was probably a special working, the engine resplendent in a smart black livery with the bogies and roof being painted white – it certainly would not stay that way for long!

J.H. Meredith

One of the first withdrawals of the 'Merchant Navy' class in 1964 was No. 35002 *Union Castle*, seen here at Vauxhall in May 1963 light engine from Nine Elms to Waterloo.

Collection of Ian Shawyer

A panoramic view of Waterloo on 29.8.66 with No. 35030 *Elder Dempster Lines* departing on the down 'Bournemouth Belle' – the 12.30 p.m. service. From this angle the area covered by the 21 platforms can be gauged, while out of sight to the left, beyond the signalbox are a number of storage sidings, including one with a lifting bridge of rail allowing rolling stock on the Waterloo and City underground section to be brought to the surface as required.

J.D. Gomersall

The line into Waterloo was carried on arches for a considerable distance out of the terminus, which was necessary due to the expanse of development right up to the railway's edge. Many of these arches have stood unaltered for almost 140 years, although changes are now imminent with the development of part of the site in connection with the Channel Tunnel.

J.D. Gomersall

61

Sunshine and shadows inside Nine Elms depôt, with a brace of 'Merchant Navys', Nos. 35001 and 35003 in company with a 'Q1' and BR standard. The engine shed here closed with the cessation of steam working and the whole site was sold for redevelopment as the new Covent Garden market.

Cedric Spiller

Slowly crossing the diamonds and points at the entrance to Waterloo Station, the Eastleigh crew of a 'Bulleid Pacific' cautiously guide their locomotive to a gentle stop a few feet from the buffers at No. 8 platform.

Now their work is partly done and there is time to watch as passengers disgorge themselves from the train to hurry past on their way to the ticket barrier. Despite having seen the sight perhaps a hundred times before there is still a thought in the minds of both men. Where do all these people go? Businessmen with 'brollies and briefcases, ladies with shopping baskets, and others who appear totally bewildered. It is also a matter of sadness to both men that few ever stop for a chat on passing the engine, but having arrived safely at their destination why should they?

After a few seconds breather driver and fireman busy themselves on the footplate, the fireman in preventing the engine from blowing off while the driver goes round checking the bearings for any sign of overheating as well as ensuring that there is still sufficient oil in the reservoirs for the short journey back to Nine Elms depôt.

For the fireman to allow the engine to blow off steam whilst stationary was a cardinal sin. Therefore, the junior member of the crew used the long shovel to move the live fire to the sides of the box so revealing an accumulation of clinker ready for disposal a little later. This had the effect of cooling the fire, for there were always plenty of inspectors around ready to jump on a young fireman should the safety valves start to lift.

With the engine now simmering quietly the 'pep pipe' is turned on to spray the coal in the tender and damp down the dust ready for the reverse run to the shed.

The Waterloo shunter arrives, a short man in the greasiest of overalls, but with a shiny peaked cap worn at an angle which appears to defy gravity. The grease from dozens of oily couplings handled during the shift was evidently sufficient to secure the hat in the desired place.

'Alright to unhook driver, we're on the other end . . . .,' calls the shunter and so in response the driver winds the reverser into back gear and eases back gently to release the pressure on the couplings. 'Right-away,' calls a voice and so checking that the platform indicator shows 'off' the engine slowly moves back against the train which is now being pulled by another engine from the other end.

On reaching the end of the platform the brakes are applied and the crew wait for the 'dolly' which will allow them to run main line to Nine Elms.

There is no time for idling at Waterloo, so as soon as the signal shows clear the driver opens up the regulator and to the sound of a variety of staccato beats the engine moves sharply away to clatter over pointwork in the direction from which it has just come.

If they had time to look the crew would see a number of young boys, and the not so young, busily scribbling on their notepads. These are some of the few who stop to watch the engines' passage, as on the roads below the viaduct such movement hardly warrants a second glance – an everyday scene, witnessed countless times already that day.

Now the reason for damping the coal becomes clear, as tender first running causes the dust to blow around, so much so that the driver soon moans about the state of his shoes and reaching for a cloth makes an attempt to restore the shine in evidence a few moments earlier.

Past Vauxhall and the sweet and sickly smell of beef-tea emanating from the factory and the engine is soon slowing for 'The Junction' and the entrance to the depôt. After a brief halt the signal changes permitting a cautious approach to the shed, the Eastleigh men being well aware of other more unfortunate colleagues who approached the shed too fast only to find another engine moving across their path.

Cautiously the 'Bulleid' takes her place in the queue for the coal hopper. Help is at hand in the shape of two Nine Elms stalwarts who will take over the engine while it is at the depôt, allowing the Eastleigh crew to take their meal break.

Glad of the rest the Eastleigh crew are quickly off the engine and out of the gate, the canteen being given a wide berth in favour of the local pub a few yards distant.

The 'local' for the railwaymen was 'The Brook', which took its name from the appropriately named Brooklands Road. Facing the brown-painted gates of the steam depôt was the door to the public bar, and on a hot day an oasis to hot and thirsty loco men.

Behind the bar was 'Arry who had a reputation as one of the most belligerent and ill-mannered landlords anywhere. Railwaymen were tolerated in his pub only because he needed their money but as for offering a welcome – that was impossible. However, the beer was beautiful and the first pint did not touch the sides, so due allowance was made for the surroundings and company.

It was said that what made the ale so attractive was the underground stream running though the pub cellar so keeping the beer at just the right temperature. Consequently, it was tenpence well spent.

Besides 'Arry, another character in the steam shed who also frequented the pub and became almost a legend was 'Old Mud'. He was a driver who enjoyed buying drinks for all the ladies on pay day. So it was that Thursday's would find the bar full of females aged from 20 to 80, most complete with a flat cap and scarf! 'Drinks for the ladies . . . .' Mud would call and his hard earned wages would disappear like ice melting in the sun. But he came back for more, it was the same routine every week.

Meanwhile the Eastleigh men having finished their drink and consumed their sandwiches at a dusty table in the corner got up to leave. Thirty minutes was all that was allowed for their break and it was now time to make their way back to the engine ready for the return working.

Back at the depôt all is ready for them and they are soon away to Waterloo again ready for the return duty. Again it is the same greasy shunter who couples up and this time another engine will be at the back to help push the stock out and start the train moving – another turn to Waterloo completed.

Hugh Abbinnett

Towards the end of steam a number of engines had their smokebox door hinges picked out in white. No. 34104 *Bere Alston* was so treated and seen here amidst the debris outside Nine Elms shed in March 1962.

M.N.L.P.S.

To the occupants of the flats adjoining the steam depôt, engines can have have been little more than an unmitigated nuisance. This particular view of No. 34019 *Bideford* shows just how close the residential accommodation was to the engines themselves. Visible on the left, the long, low building is the shed canteen, with the area again a sea of ash and clinker.

Collection of Ian Shawyer

Almost the end at Nine Elms, depicted in June 1967 with what was formerly No. 34025 *Whinple* outside the elevated coal hopper. In the background is the preserved 'A4' *Sir Nigel Gresley* saved from the cutters torch. No. 34025 would not be so lucky.

D. MacKinnon

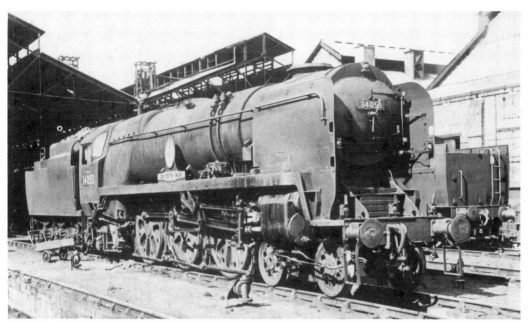

Outside the 'new' shed at Nine Elms in September 1965 is the rebuilt 'Battle of Britain' and No. 34053 *Sir Keith Park*. Shortly after the photograph was taken the engine worked to Eastleigh on a parcels train and was withdrawn upon its arrival – for no other reason than that the accountants required a set number of steam withdrawals that week.

M.N.L.P.S.

Another of the BR Class '5s' allocated to the Southern Region, No. 73115 *King Pellinore* seen outside the 'old' shed at Nine Elms. Despite having some 140 Pacifics on the SR the unreliability of the Bulleid class meant it was necessary to retain a number of the Standard's to cover for the duties involved. Indeed over the years some drivers came to prefer the Class 5 despite their reputation for harsh riding. A number survived right to the very end of steam on the SR, 9.7.67.

M.N.L.P.S.

A striking view of No. 35013 *Blue Funnel* alongside the coaling stage at Nine Elms. The engine had just arrived at the depôt after working a Sunday afternoon Bournemouth to Waterloo service. It would then be coaled and watered before being made ready for its next trip. Note also the line up of diesel shunters in the background.

Cedric Spiller

No. 35013 was certainly a well photographed engine as here she is again leaning to the curve at Clapham Junction with the 1.30 p.m. Waterloo to Bournemouth and Weymouth on Saturday 28.5.66.

J.D. Gomersall

Travelling in the opposite direction was a shockingly dirty No. 34096 *Trevone* on a passenger working from Salisbury. The slow speed dictated by the curves at Clapham Junction made this location a favourite with photographers and it was not unusual for as many as 50 to congregate at any one particular time.

Collection of A.J. Fry

Westwards now to Woking, with No. 35007 *Aberdeen Commonwealth* leaving a trail of black smoke as it arrives at the station on a down West of England train. Behind the tender the first coach carries the set number '951' which followed the SR practice of permanently coupling vehicles together in rakes according to their type.

R.N. Joanes

An unusual sight at Woking, the original LMS diesel-electric No. 10000 of 1947. This engine along with her sister No. 10001, were allocated to the Southern Region for a brief period in 1951 and put to use on the main line services to Weymouth and Exeter. Despite it being a representative of more modern motive power the whole exterior appears today to be decidedly dated, although its performance (along with that of the three SR main line diesels), was such as to convince BR that this was the means of replacing steam working.

Collection of Ian Shawyer

Woking with a more conventional visitor for the period, No. 35010 *Blue Star* on a non-stop Bournemouth line express in May 1966.

J.D. Gomersall

Probably the most famous of all the trains to run on the Southern was the 'Golden Arrow', seen here at Victoria awaiting departure just prior to nationalisation. At the head is No. 21C119, later No. 34019 *Bideford*, and carrying a livery of malachite green, highlighted by three bands of yellow. The insignia is of particular interest and consists of the flags of Great Britain and France as well as the well-known headboard. A little later it was also the practice to carry two large arrows on the side of the engine.

Lens of Sutton

One of the dreaded Oxted line steam workings about to depart from Victoria. At the head is a powerful Class '4' tank, No. 80088, although even this would have been hard pushed to keep out of the way of the electric units which would share the same route for part of the journey. Victoria had gone over almost entirely to electric traction following the Kent Coast electrification schemes although, like the services to Oxted, there remained pockets of steam working for some time afterwards.

Derek Clayton

Clapham Junction this time and a panoramic view from the footbridge looking west to the Richmond lines. Part of the vast array of yardage is also visible with at least three steam engines to be seen. No. 30454 *Queen Quinevere* is possibly on a freight from Feltham.

Derek Clayton

Apart from the main line to Weymouth another steam working persisted in the centre of London almost to the very end. This was the Clapham Junction–Kensington Olympia shuttle. No. 80015 bereft of front numberplate at Clapham Junction after working the 5.36 p.m. from Olympia on 1.5.67.

Lens of Sutton

Kensington was sited on the West London Joint Railway and so features in more than one section in this book. In this particular view ex-LBSCR 'C2X' No. 32547 is in the process of shunting at Addison Road in 1957, with the renowned frontage of Earls Court in the background.

Derek Clayton

The same engine, although the date is two years later in May 1959. No. 32547 at the head of a milk train approaching 'Olympia with the London Transport electrified lines alongside.

Derek Clayton

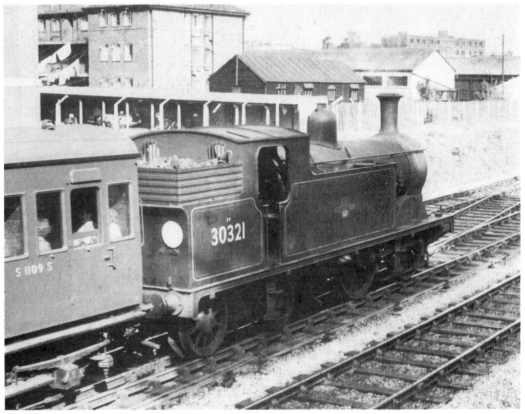

Before their withdrawal the 'M7s' had also been used on the Kensington shuttle service. No. 30321 at the head of what is perhaps a capacity service in May 1959.

Derek Clayton

A final view of Kensington, as Wainwright 'H' class 0-4-4T leaves the station with six vehicles in tow. In the background is an LT underground unit on a District line service.

Les Elsey

The principal steam shed for the Central line section of the SR was at Stewarts Lane and could be seen from the western section main line not far from Nine Elms. It was located against the backcloth of the imposing depository, which has over the years performed a variety of roles including Hampton & Sons furniture depository, then Decca Ltd, before reverting to its current use as a storage area again. In the shed yard 'P' class 0-6-0 No. 31655 is seen with the full 'British Railways' lettering on the side tanks.

W. Gilburt

Close up of an 'H' class tank at Stewarts Lane in 1950. No. 31184 in plain unlined black and with the small BR 'cycling lion' insignia.

W. Gilburt

A Southern veteran, 'D' class No. 1732 (later No. 31732) at Stewarts Lane, 10.6.50. The fireman can be seen perched at a precarious angle on the tender as the tank is refilled with water. Nowadays legislation would protect or prohibit such work; at that time there was little to assist the men, indeed it is a wonder accidents were so few.

W. Gilburt

'N' class 2-6-0 No. 31404 outside the shed in 1950. From the stains radiating from the mud-hole plugs, the engine had recently had its boiler washed out, an occasional but vital task, but necessary if steaming was not to be impaired.

W. Gilburt

Another named train from Victoria was the London–Paris 'Night Ferry', with the engine for that duty, No. 35029 *Ellerman Lines* being prepared for the task. 14.4.51.

Les Elsey

Stewarts Lane depôt remains open today, even if sights like this are unfortunately no longer part of the everyday scene. No. 34005 *Barnstaple* – the first 'West Country' to be rebuilt, outside the shed awaiting its next duty.

Collection of Ian Shawyer

There are several examples of Bulleid's work now preserved including No. 34101 *Hartland Point*, seen here at the Lane prior to rebuilding. The Bulleid designed wheels show up particularly well in this view and were intended to serve a dual function as a means of securing a better contact with the tyre as well as a saving in weight compared with a conventional spoked assembly.

W. Gilburt

At the head of a passenger working from Charing Cross is 'N15' 4-6-0 No. 30804 *Sir Cador of Cornwall*. The 'King Arthur' class were largely made redundant as a result of the electrification of the lines into Kent; for at the same time as they were piling up in the sheds on the western section, a veritable army of Bulleid Pacifics were sharing the same fate. Unfortunately, there was insufficient work for such an influx of engines and the 'King Arthur' class were relegated to menial tasks and then withdrawn with no suitable work left for them.

Roger Sherlock

Referred to briefly in the introduction to the SR section, this is the remains of the connection linking the two Waterloo stations as seen from the South Eastern side. It is indeed a pity that such a facility does not still exist today, for the opportunities for through workings would surely be of benefit to the traveller.

Lens of Sutton

Despite being primarily a passenger railway the SR did of course handle freight and parcels. One of the latter services is shown here with a superbly proportioned 'D1' 4-4-0, No. 31507 at the head of a mixed rake of SR design utility vans.

Les Elsey

The shed at Hither Green dealt mainly with engines on freight workings and shunting turns. Here one of the big 'W' class tanks is seen at rest between duties. These three-cylinder monsters were seen on a variety of turns although most of their work was involved in yard and trip working within the London area. Rarely, if ever, did they work a passenger service, a throw back to the Sevenoaks derailment of 1927, when a tank engine (not a 'W') left the rails at speed resulting in a considerable loss of life. From that time on, the SR had a fear of working passenger trains using a large tank engine class.

W. Gilburt

Temporarily resident at Hither Green is ex-LNER 'J17', No. 65536, once a regular feature of the SR scene in London on a freight working from its home territory. 14.4.51.

Les Elsey

82

As a replacement for steam shunting within the various marshalling yards the 350 hp diesel shunters were introduced. Indeed many remain in service today, with the basic design little altered from that seen here. This is No. 13049 at Hither Green, another pair of the same type can be seen in the background.

W. Gilburt

For a while during the 1950s the SR made use of a number of the Riddles design 'Austerity' 2-8-0s. No. 90562 in remarkably clean condition at Hither Green in 1950. Notice the unusual headcode as well as the solid centre to the front bogie wheels. Of the 732 engines in the class all were claimed by the scrap-merchants and none survived into preservation.

W. Gilburt

By 1951 there were only two remaining Marsh 'H1' 'Atlantics' in service and already due for early withdrawal. This is No. 32037 *Selsey Bill*, seen at Bricklayers Arms depôt in South London and in steam awaiting its next duty. Notice the three pipes on the front buffer beam, for steam heating, vacuum and air brakes.

W. Gilburt

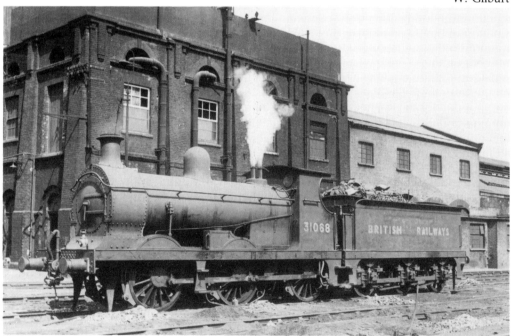

The 'C' class engines were built for through freight working on the SECR, although as loads increased they were relegated to lesser duties. Even so most survived nationalisation with three ending their days as shunters at Ashford works (Kent). This is No. 31068 in ordinary service, seen at Bricklayers Arms depôt in 1950.

W. Gilburt

Slightly smaller than the 'C's were the similar 'O1' class, but in this case few survived into BR ownership. No. 1066 is seen here in store at New Cross Gate shed, a favourite location for engines out of service in this way. (No. 1066 was eventually renumbered by BR as 31066.)

W. Gilburt

Steam shunting at New Cross, 'E6' 0-6-2T displaying an early form of BR numbering with small figures in 1950. This was a design of locomotive associated with the former Central section, although following the grouping in 1923 it was the practice to despatch engines to where they were needed most and not always to their home territory.

W. Gilburt

'Leader' No. 36002 in store at New Cross, 23.6.51. This was the second engine in this ill-fated class and although virtually complete it was never steamed. She was towed to Brighton and the cutters torch the day after the photograph was taken. (More information on the 'Leader' story is given in my book *Leader – Steam's Last Chance*.)

Brian Morrison

A seldom photographed and an apparently little known machine was No. 11001, a diesel shunter to the characteristic design of O.V.S. Bulleid. Built at Ashford the engine entered service with the SR in 1946. Intended to be suitable for both shunting and branch line work, the machine failed to come up to expectations, mainly because of gear box trouble. It was withdrawn in 1959.

W. Gilburt

Concluding our brief look at SR in the London area is this view of Beattie 'well tanks' Nos. 30585 and 30587 on a joint RCTS/SLS railtour at Hampton Court on 2.12.62. The pair, along with a sister engine, No. 30586, were the survivors of a numerous class once used on the London suburban workings. Most were rendered redundant at a very early stage following the electrification of the services they worked. These three survivors had been retained for working the Wenford Bridge mineral branch in Cornwall, but by 1962 modernisation had reached even this far flung outpost and they were on their way to Eastleigh and withdrawal. Fortunately two survived into preservation.

Roger Sherlock

The Eastern Region

When speaking about the present day Eastern Region of British Railways, one is in fact referring to the successor to the London & North Eastern Railway; which was itself a combination of the Great Northern, North Eastern, Great Eastern and Great Central companies as well as a number of smaller concerns operating in Scotland.

Without a doubt the best known of all the ER lines must be that from London to Edinburgh and so it is at the starting point for this famous line at Kings Cross that our brief outline will begin.

However, before referring to the railway on the site, mention should be made to the legend which has it that Queen Boadicea fought her last battle against the Romans on land now occupied by the station and that she lies buried somewhere beneath Platform 8. Be that as it may, Kings Cross had opened as late as 1852, originally with just one arrival and departure platform separated by no less than 14 sidings. Covering these tracks was a twin-arched roof having a 71ft. span, built to the design of Lewis Cubitt using the same principles of construction as that employed in the Tsar's riding school in Moscow.

Busy times at Kings Cross, when commuters into London regularly used the train long before the motor car age of today.

'R.A.' Collection

The original Potters Bar station on the Great Northern line out of Kings Cross. The number of staff visible (at least 9) are a reminder of days when labour was both cheap and plentiful.

Lens of Sutton

The original Euston, St Pancras and Kings Cross stations were all sited within a short distance of each other and therefore present an interesting contrast in architectural styles. This could also be taken as a representation of the prevailing state of the economy at the time each was built. Thus the first two stations were conspicuous by their decor, while Kings Cross is strikingly frugal.

Such appearances were not helped in the early years by an infrequent train service from Kings Cross, for example in 1855 there were just 19 departures daily. But this steadily grew over the years so that by 1875 it was necessary to open a new suburban station alongside the original terminal. A few years later in 1892–3 the accommodation was again increased, this time with a number of new platforms which replaced certain of the covered sidings. The curve from the steep single line leading to the Metropolitan Railway (No. 16) was also eased at the same time. This was more commonly known as the 'Hotel Curve'. From a suitable vantage point one could watch a struggling steam engine emerge 'from the depths' onto the 'Hotel Curve' at regular intervals before pausing to collect its train load of passengers. Pulling away was another difficult operation accompanied by frantically spinning wheels and columns of smoke as the crew valiantly fought to bring their train back under control. Those with cameras perched at the north end of the station would watch such displays with scant attention preferring instead to focus on the main line services, usually one of the magnificent 'A4' Pacifics.

From the late 1930s and for almost a quarter of a century, Sir Nigel Gresley's 'A4' design captured the imagination of young and old alike, particularly whenever speeds were mentioned. How this came about can easily be explained, for as all school-boys knew it was an engine called *Mallard* which had captured the world speed record for steam traction at 126 m.p.h. in July 1938 and it was one of the 'A4' class of engines. We were taught to be proud to be British – it is one of the few records that is unlikely ever to be beaten.

We have digressed slightly in speaking of engines but no matter, for it seemed the public admired the names adorning the express passenger engines. *Golden Fleece, Wild Swan, Gannet* and *Kingfisher* all conjured up visions of graceful speed. At the opposite end of the scale some of the other ER Pacifics carried the names of famous racehorses, *Pretty Polly* and *Blink Bonny* seemed somehow not in quite the same league.

Leaving Kings Cross the line plunged almost immediately into the delightfully named Copenhagen Tunnel, followed by the not so delightful but equally descriptive Gasworks Tunnel. Between the two a connecton led off to the Royal Mint Street Station which was close by the terminus at Fenchurch Street. While the tunnels themselves may attract no more than a passing glimpse from the travelling passenger, the railway and residential area surrounding them was immortalised a few years ago in the classic Ealing comedy *The Ladykillers*. North from the tunnels come the massive shunting yards at Finsbury Park, followed by stations at Wood Green, New Southgate, Hadley Wood and Potters Bar. Potters Bar station was rebuilt by BR in the late 1950s as the model for an urban stopping place of the future. Unfortunately rapidly changing architectural styles have made the whole appearance seem dated, whilst the use of concrete and plastics have also aged badly in the ensuing years.

Fenchurch Street is a much older terminal than Kings Cross having opened back in 1841. It was the starting point for services on a number of the Great Eastern lines into Essex, as well as serving the docks and wharfs on the north side of the Thames. As briefly referred to in the Midland Region section, it has also been used as the terminal for trains on the line to Tilbury, Southend and Shoeburyness since electrification of that route in 1962.

Apart from Fenchurch Street, the influence of the Great Eastern was mostly felt at their main terminal of Liverpool Street. This was another recent station, (in terms of

Suburban steam at Seven Sisters station in LNER days. The engine is an 'F7' tank of 1909 vintage which were known as 'Crystal Palace' tanks owing to their large windowed cabs.

Lens of Sutton

railway history, London stations opened after 1860 are termed recent) and was first used in 1874. It replaced the inconveniently sited GER station at Bishopsgate. From Liverpool Street the GER operated a network of lines into the East Anglia area as well as a vast network of routes through suburban Essex.

Northeast of the Liverpool Street terminus, the GER established at Stratford a workshop, locomotive depôt and marshalling yards, the whole complex is still an important part of the nationalised network today.

Saddest of all the London terminals must be that at Marylebone, situated towards the northwest of the capital between Euston and Paddington. How such a station came to be under the control of the LNER is a story which could rightly occupy many pages but, briefly, it may be said that this occurred as a result of the takeover of the Great Central Company by the LNER in 1923.

The Great Central was perhaps better known as the last main line into London. The route commenced at Sheffield before running south through Nottingham and Leicester, before reaching Aylesbury and eventually the capital. In addition there was a joint line with the GWR through High Wycombe, as well as favourable relations with the Metropolitan Railway Company.

Marylebone had opened in 1899, a bold attempt by an independent company to challenge the monopoly of the rival railway companies with regard to traffic into Buckinghamshire and beyond. In appearance the station presented a mock-tudor façade, arguably more akin to a provincial station rather than an important London terminal. But in keeping with the best railway tradition an imposing hotel was erected alongside, although who used its high panelled rooms is open to question.

Marylebone's heyday was really the Edwardian era, for this was the time when the green fields of Buckingham and Hertford were being ploughed up for housing as it became one of the most desirable places to live within easy reach of the capital. The GCR had the foresight to see this expansion coming and responded with fast and frequent peak hour services, including dining car trains from as close as Rickmansworth and Aylesbury. To the inhabitants of both towns this must have been marvellous, especially when Aylesbury had in the past been little more than the terminus of a nondescript GWR branch line from Princes Risborough.

Who having seen John Betjeman's superb rendition about the development of the area can ever forget his *Metroland*?

Unfortunately, such success for the GCR near to London was not matched by equal success elsewhere. So with the pruning of the BR network the whole of the former GCR main line was slowly run down and then closed, leaving Marylebone as a shameful reminder of past glories. Since those sad days of the 1960s the only services regularly leaving the station are a handful of local trains, ironically to the same suburban outlands, although now the restaurant cars are no more, replaced by nondescript diesel units.

The very fact that Marylebone has at times been under the control of the Western, Midland and Eastern regions leads to the impression of an unwanted station, although the presence of the BR Board headquarters in the former GCR Hotel since 1948 has at least been one form of stability. But now there are plans to re-locate the Board to some vacant offices at Paddington and so once again the future of the whole site must be in doubt.

At Kings Cross, Liverpool Street and Fenchurch Street it is the electric train that now rules the day. Marylebone, however, is unlikely to see such progress as squeezed by its larger neighbours from the outset it was never able to develop as was hoped. Like the steam engine itself it can only vainly hope for a return to past glories.

LONDON. TRAIN FERRY Nº3.

HARWICH - ZEEBRUGGE TRAIN FERRY
THROUGH TRUCK SERVICE DAILY
SAVES PACKING HANDLING & TIME
FULL PARTICULARS FROM GREAT EASTERN TRAIN FERRIES LTD
III HAMILTON HOUSE   155 BISHOPSGATE   LONDON E C 2

Sheffield
Nottingham

MARYLEBONE

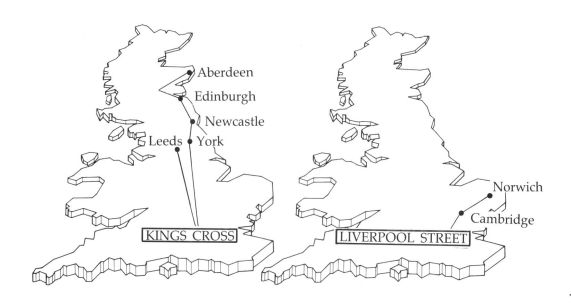

Aberdeen

Edinburgh

Newcastle

Leeds • York

KINGS CROSS

Norwich

Cambridge

LIVERPOOL STREET

What better way to start our brief look at the Eastern Region steam than with an immaculate 'A4' Pacific? No. 60028 *Walter K. Whigham* pulling out of Kings Cross on a Royal train special working during 1961.

'R.A.' Collection

At the other end of the station 'A3' Pacific, No. 60056 *Centenary* rests after arriving with an up express on 21.10.61. The 'A3' class were derived from Sir Nigel Gresley's first Pacific design and 79 were built from 1922 onwards.

M. Mensing

A 'V2' and a 'Pacific' shunt back into Kings Cross station, probably from the depôt at Top Shed. Its proximity to the neighbouring St Pancras station can be gauged by the curved roof of the adjacent terminal which can be seen above the platform canopy.

Derek Clayton

Shunting at Kings Cross was usually carried out by a variety of tank engines, the 'N2' class were some of the most prolific. On 31.1.59 No. 69539 is coupled onto the empty stock of the 9.55 a.m. ex-Newcastle and awaits the signal to proceed. The engine is fitted with condensing apparatus for working on the 'Hotel Curve' line.

M. Mensing

An impressive view of 'A1' No. 60148 *Aboyeur* at the terminus in June 1962. At that time this was a Leeds, Copley Hill engine and so had probably arrived in London on an express from the north. The 'A1' class had a comparatively short life span, with a number not coming into service until after BR had been formed. Dieselisation rendered them redundant and all were withdrawn despite having years of useful life left, none survived into preservation.

Roger Sherlock

Another 'A3', this time without smoke deflectors. Indeed apart from the livery and double chimney, No. 60102 *Sir Frederick Banbury* is in near original condition. The white streaks on the firebox side are an indication of a recent boiler washout. As with the former GWR engines, most of which bore a family resemblance, so the LNER machines had a common trait, that of a curved top to the cabside windows, seen here to advantage.

Roger Sherlock

A different 'A1' this time, No. 60130 *Kestral* awaiting departure time from Kings Cross. LNER policy for naming engines covered two main themes, racehorses and birds, the latter a pleasing feature which seemed appropriate on the engines concerned.

Roger Sherlock

Stranger in the camp, an ex-LMS 'Duchess', No. 46245 *City of London* outside Kings Cross ready for a special working in June 1963. Locomotive enthusiasts have for long argued the merits of a 'Duchess' against an 'A4' with regard to maximum speed, especially when the former LMS-type were in their original streamlined condition. It is unlikely now that we shall ever know if *Mallard's* record could have been broken.

Roger Sherlock

The peak years for the holiday camp-type of vacation were in the 1950s and it was not unnatural that BR should get involved with the running of special trains to the resorts concerned. Accordingly on 7.6.58, 'B1' 4-6-0 was at the head of a 'Butlins Express' to Skegness seen just departing from Kings Cross.

'R.A.' Collection

Apart from the first photograph in this section, no record of Kings Cross would be complete without some views of the 'A4s' in normal service. In doing so I have attempted to choose engines not often seen on film, No. 60030 *Golden Fleece* and No. 60032 *Gannet* at the head of their respective expresses, 'The Elizabethan' and 'The Northumbrian'. In both cases notice the clean condition of the engines which even extends to the front coupling. The policy of painting the engine class on the streamlined casing between the buffers is also visible.

'R.A.' Collection

To draw comparisons with the previous views here are two shots of the 'Deltic' diesels which replaced steam on front line Eastern Region duties from 1961. At the time of their introduction these engines were scorned by the enthusiast, yet when they were withdrawn 20 years later in favour of the HST sets such was their following that a number passed into preservation. On the left is No. D9003 *Meld* at the head of special press trip in July 1961, with sister engine No. D9001 (later named *St. Paddy*) alongside.

'R.A.' Collection

For general duties on the LNER system, Gresley had introduced his 'K3' class in 1924. This is No. 61838 at Kings Cross steam shed in 1954 with another distinctive trait of LNER steam design – the smokebox door, clearly visible.

W. Gilburt

Only eight members of the 184 strong 'V2' class were named with No. 60847 *St. Peter's School York A.D. 627* perhaps the best known. The 'V2' design was without doubt a remarkably versatile machine, capable of hauling anything from heavy goods to fast passenger services and having the same power output as the larger 'A3' class. No. 60847 is seen against a background of several other steam types at Kings Cross shed in May 1963.

Roger Sherlock

As a modern replacement for the 'N2' class, Gresley's successor, Edward Thompson designed the 'L1' type of large tank engine, No. 67779 is shown at Kings Cross in 1954. Successful as they undoubtably were, they never completely ousted the earlier machines from suburban duties and consequently both types worked hand-in-hand almost to the very end. The class were another early casualty of the modernisation programme and most were withdrawn from service simply because no further work could be found for them.

W. Gilburt

Besides carrying names of rather doubtful suitability, a number of the 'A3s' were fitted with German-type smoke deflectors late in their life. An improvement or disfigurement according to personal taste. This is a Kings Cross based machine, No. 60039 *Sandwich* near the coaling stage at its home shed in July 1962.

Roger Sherlock

Another Kings Cross engine was 'A1' No. 60158 *Aberdonian* in a relatively clean condition as late as May 1963. By this time steam had already been largely superseded by diesel on main line passenger workings and so No. 60158 may well have been in steam as a stand-by to cover for a possible diesel failure.

Roger Sherlock

To conclude our look at Kings Cross what better way to end than with the now preserved 'A4' *Sir Nigel Gresley* depicted on shed in 1963. To many crews, No. 7, as she was known, was one of the best of the class, an exceptionally fast and free steaming machine. It is a pity that she was not given the opportunity to see if *Mallard's* 126 m.p.h. could have been beaten.

Roger Sherlock

North of Kings Cross is Hornsey and the site of a large goods yard. Prior to the introduction of the diesel shunters it was serviced by steam tanks, the poor visibility from these engines being apparent from the photograph.

'R.A.' Collection

Another view taken in Hornsey yard and this time a new 'Brush' Type 2 diesel, No. D5654. A considerable variety of signals can also be seen, most of which are ex-Great Northern types although by this time modified with upper quadrant fittings.

'R.A.' Collection

With steam on and the fireman working hard, No. 60013 *Dominion of New Zealand* speeds past Wood Green with the afternoon 'Talisman' express on 19.6.57.

'R.A.' Collection

For many years the LNER maintained one particular engine for working royal trains bound for Sandringham, 'B17' No. 61671 *Royal Sovereign* being the selected engine. Here, though, it is seen in normal service passing Wood Green on a Cambridge to Kings Cross working. The first vehicle is still in LNER varnished teak livery. A further view of No. 61671 is on p. 120.

'R.A.' Collection

Probably the most famous train of all, the 'Flying Scotsman', in the charge of No. 60136 *Alcazar* leaving Hadley Wood South tunnel with the down or northbound working. To add confusion to the photograph it must also be remembered that there was also an engine bearing the same name as the train involved which can be seen regularly today working special services in a variety of locations throughout mainland Britain.

'R.A.' Collection

Aside from the main line express services it is important to remember that the east coast main line was also very busy with freight. A typical service shown here near Potters Bar with Riddles 'Austerity' 2-8-0, No. 90093 in charge of a train of mineral wagons.

W. Gilburt

Running under Class 'A' or express headcodes, 'L1' class 2-6-4T No. 67741 is in charge of an outer suburban train made up of two 4-car sets of articulated stock.

W. Gilburt

A pleasing gesture was the naming of three members of the 'A1' class after the constituent companies of the LNER. One was No. 60157 *Great Eastern* seen here in charge of an express near Potters Bar in the early 1950s. At this time approval had been given to quadruple the main line in this area and an early stage of this work is in progress alongside the running lines.

W. Gilburt

On the last leg of its journey south from Leeds, 'A3' No. 60047 *Donovan* hurries along the four track section of main line near Brookmans Park with the 7.28 a.m. to Kings Cross on 4.8.53. The train would appear to consist of a mixed selection of vehicles and with an ex-Great Northern coach second from the tender.

'R.A.' Collection

No. 60032 *Gannet* at the head of a down express. The tender would appear to be laden with a good selection of coal which could make all the difference to the timekeeping on a long run. Underneath the cab the escaping steam is an indication that the fireman may be attempting to get the injector to work, although he appears to be nonchalantly gazing at the scenery rather than concentrating on putting water into the boiler.

W. Gilburt

Signs of the new order as No. D5313 hurries through Brookmans Park with an outer suburban working. As with the earlier photograph on p. 108 the train is made up of articulated coaching stock with just five bogies supporting each set of four vehicles.

'R.A.' Collection

A 'Baby Deltic' at the head of a Cambridge buffet train in July 1959. Despite early promise these engines proved to be unreliable in service and so were destined to have a far shorter lifespan than the steam engines they replaced.

'R.A.' Collection

Besides working the fast express services to the north, the 'A4s' were also occasionally employed on the Cambridge line services. No. 60013 *Dominion of New Zealand* recorded by the camera on the 10.40 a.m. Cambridge to Kings Cross near Brookmans Park in 1953.

'R.A.' Collection

To conclude our look at the Great Northern main line from Kings Cross what better than an 'N2' in full flight. No. 69506 at the head of a Kings Cross–Welwyn Garden City outer suburban service in June 1954.

'R.A.' Collection

The reason for fitting a number of the 'A3s' with smoke deflectors was the perennial difficulty of drifting smoke obscuring the forward vision. The new adornments are apparently only partly successful on No. 60047 as it leaves a trail of steam behind on an express near to Hadley Wood in the last days of steam working from Kings Cross.

Les Elsey

At a more sedate pace when compared with the previous train a Class 9, No. 92148 rumbles along with 50 mineral wagons in tow bound for the London yards.

Les Elsey

We turn now to the former Great Eastern lines and their terminus at Liverpool Street, a station which has run at almost peak capacity for many years now and is perhaps typified by this 1950s view. I particularly like the group of passengers with their luggage; certainly the fashions of the day are worthy of close study.

Lens of Sutton

The 'N2s' also worked a number of the steam suburban services from Liverpool Street and to destinations like Chingford and Bishops Stortford. Here two members of the class, Nos. 69656 and 69724 are poised under the recently erected overhead wires, with No. 67706 in the background.

Lens of Sutton

Supplementing the 'N2' class on the suburban services from Liverpool Street were the smaller 'J69' class. Both types were fitted with Westinghouse air compressors of the type shown here. Despite their small size these remarkable little engines performed prodigious feats of speed and weight haulage and were only superseded by the advent of more modern types of traction. Another view of this engine before being renumbered is shown later in this section.

Roger Sherlock

The empty stock of a train from Norwich about to be moved out of the terminus by 'B1' 4-6-0 No. 61254 on 21.3.59.

M. Mensing

116

One of the earliest twinnings between English towns and others abroad occurred in 1951 when Boston, Lincolnshire was twinned with Boston, USA. To commemorate the event a 'B1' 4-6-0, No. 61379 was named *Mayflower*, and is seen here at Liverpool Street along with representatives of both communities. The engine also carried a commemorative plate on the cabside which bore the following inscription;

'This locomotive was named Mayflower
13 July 1951 as a symbol of the ties
binding the two towns of Boston
and of the lasting friendship
between the U.S.A. and the
British Commonwealth'

'R.A.' Collection

Among the early casualties of modernisation were the 'B17' 4-6-0s, although to be fair many had a reputation for very rough riding. Perhaps this was the reason for No. 61632 *Belvoir Castle* being relegated to a stopping passenger service, seen here awaiting departure at Liverpool Street in the early 1950s.

Les Elsey

For a short while BR experimented with a Mk.1 coach modified with an 'auto-buffet' much like a modern vending machine. The idea was to reduce costs by dispensing with catering staff on trains and the venture was tried out on a number of routes including the Norwich line services. It failed for two reasons, firstly the public objected to the impersonal service a machine could offer and the whole concept was also easy prey to vandals.

British Railways

The main steam depôt for Liverpool Street was at Stratford which maintained an allocation of both main line and shunting engines. This is 'B17' No. 61657 *Doncaster Rovers* outside the depôt carrying the early BR crest on the tender. The 'B17s' had been the mainstay of services on the Great Eastern lines until ousted by the 'Britannia' class, although from the appearance of No. 61657 she would appear to be spruced up ready for a main line duty.

'R.A.' Collection

Dating back to 1881, this is 'J15' No. 65432 at Stratford in May 1958. These little engines were ideal for working on some of the lighter branch lines as well as trip workings between the various London freight yards.

M.N.L.P.S.

A Gresley 'K3' No. 61880, seen at its home depôt of Stratford on 27.3.57.

Roger Sherlock

Alternative motive power for the East London railtour of 14.4.51, with ex-LMS tank No. 47300 at Stratford station complete with a crowd of admirers alongside.

Les Elsey

Royal Sovereign again, this time with its white cab roof clearly visible. The remainder of the engine would also appear to be spotlessly clean so it is interesting to speculate what working No. 61671 was on when this photograph was taken.

'R.A.' Collection

The 'up' or London bound 'Scandinavian' express passing Mountessing in July 1954 behind 'B1' No. 61004 *Oryx*. On the left the signal is an early variant of the modern colour light, with the rectangular white and black board on the post indicating that it was automatically operated.

'R.A.' Collection

One of Stratford's 'Britannia' Pacifics, No. 70039 *Sir Christopher Wren* near Mountessing with the 'East Anglian' service. The train would appear to consist of just eight vehicles most of which are to the standard LNER design with a 'bow end' to the roof.

'R.A.' Collection

Another 'Britannia' and this time No. 70037 *Hereward the Wake* at speed near Hatfield Peverel on 'The Broadsman' express. Compared with the previous view sharp eyed readers may notice the handrails have been removed from the smoke deflectors and replaced by grab holes. This was a direct result of the Milton accident on the Western Region which is referred to in detail in the companion volume *Last Days of Steam in Berkshire*.

'R.A.' Collection

A very grimy 'B1', No. 61399 east of Kelvedon (High Level) with the down 'Day Continental' service. Notice particularly the position of the train nameboard on the buffer beam – perhaps someone could not reach to locate it in the more usual spot!

'R.A.' Collection

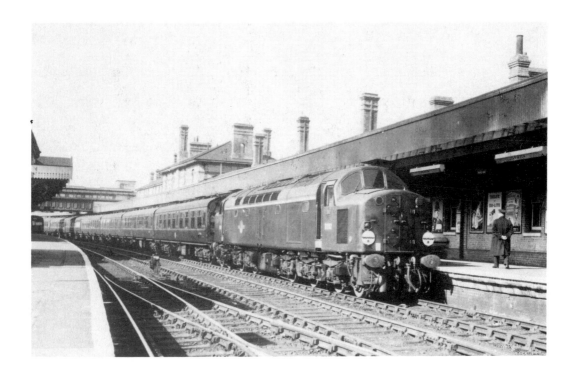

A number of diesel types were tried out to replace steam on the lines into East Anglia, the most common of these being those which later became the Class 31s and Class 40s. Here No. D202 of the latter type draws slowly to a stand at Ipswich station with a Norwich–Liverpool Street service on 15.3.60, in the background is an unidentified Class '31'.

'R.A.' Collection

Turning now to Marylebone and an 'L1' tank slowly reversing out of the station. Compared with the obvious bustle of most other London terminals, Marylebone presents a far more serene appearance. The British Railways van in the background is another reminder of days long past.

W. Gilburt

Another 'L1', No. 67768 awaiting departure from the station. I particularly like the ornate platform lamps with their scroll work which was so typical of the station and the age of steam.

W. Gilburt

Once a familiar feature on the roads and especially at stations was the Scammell 'Scarab' in its eye catching livery of red and cream. This is the 3-ton version represented by OLB 241 outside Lodge Road RME depôt, Marylebone in April 1954.

'R.A.' Collection

The 50th anniversary of The Institute of Locomotive Engineers in 1961, was marked by a special commemorative exhibition which was staged at Marylebone. Included in the display were examples of the latest rail technology as well as aspects from the past. A variety of steam types can therefore be seen.

'R.A.' Collection

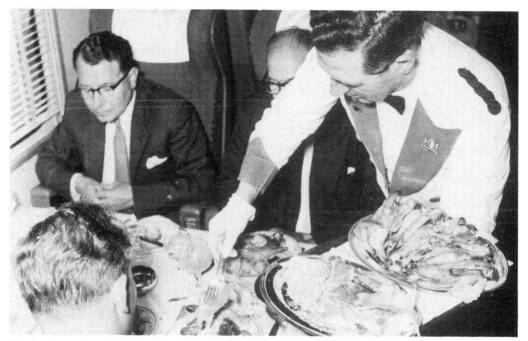

Meals at speed – table service on the short lived Marylebone–Birmingham Pullman service in 1960. The photograph is reputed to have been taken near High Wycombe so allowing it to come within the scope of coverage of this volume.

'R.A.' Collection

One of the VIP visitors to Marylebone on 12.5.61 was HRH Prince Philip, seen here descending from the cab of the solitary BR 'Class 8' Pacific, No. 71000 *Duke of Gloucester*.

'R.A.' Collection

A London terminus not covered so far is that at Fenchurch Street. To make good that ommision here is *Super Claud* No. 62613 awaiting departure from Platform 3 with an LCGB special in August 1959. Despite its outwardly good external condition there is evidence of previous heavy working, judging by the burn marks on the lower half of the smokebox door. No. 62613 was withdrawn from service not long afterwards.

Roger Sherlock

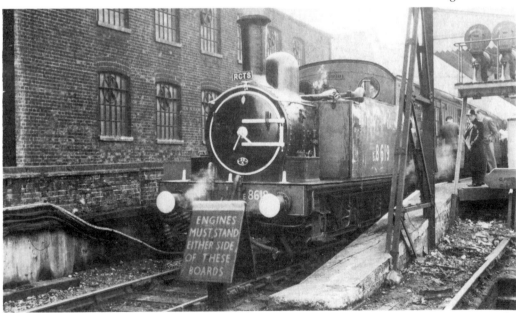

For a short while after nationalisation a number of engines from all the regions were given a single letter prefix to their old number. One example is shown here, with No. E8619, later No. 68619 at Fenchurch Street on a special working.

Les Elsey

An original LTS tank, 4-4-2, No. 41970 at Fenchurch Street in 1952. All were rendered redundant by electrification, although one has been preserved with its original '80' number and name *Thundersley*.

Les Elsey

Steam on an electrified line with 'J83' 0-6-0 No. 68450 piloting a Loughton–Eastbourne excursion near Buckhurst Hill on 19.7.53.

'R.A.' Collection

The London Midland Region

Largest of all the pre-nationalisation companies was the London Midland & Scottish Railway which operated the West Coast main lines from London, through the Midlands and parts of Wales to the very tip of Scotland at Thurso and Wick.

The LMS had been made up of several important railway companies, the London & North Western, Midland, Lancashire & Yorkshire and Furness to name but a few. (The L & Y had in fact amalgamatedwith the LNWR just prior to 1923.) Despite such a make up the LMS only operated two main line terminals in London at Euston and St Pancras, although, in addition there was also the smaller terminal at Broad Street situated off the former North London line – more about this later.

Euston must surely vie as perhaps the best known of all London stations even if today it is but a shadow of its former self with the famous Doric Arch now consigned to memory. The station itself was part of the original London and Birmingham route which had opened from Euston Square to Boxmoor in July 1837. Completion of the railway to Birmingham came just over a year later, with the company incorporated into the newly formed LNWR in 1846.

At that time the LNWR was in the forefront of railway development, its only likely rival being the GWR. Consequently the LNWR adopted the name the 'Premier Line' based on its reputation for both quality of ride and speed of traffic.

Unfortunately, such a reputation was hardly best upheld by the state of Euston station. Although, externally the Doric Arch was intended to portray a station in keeping with the importance of the City it served, inside was a conglomeration of platforms and offices in which it was not unknown for a passenger to become disorientated or even totally lost.

How this came about is worthy of mention, with the first stage of the confusion dating back to 1846 when the initial add-ons were made. All this was, of course, due to the phenomenal and totally unexpected success of railway travel.

Originally Euston had consisted of just two parallel train sheds, these were soon being demolished to be replaced eventually by no less than 15 platforms of varying lengths. Despite such facilities the track layout leading to the station was poor and it was not until well into BR days that a long overdue rebuilding programme was instigated. Sadly, in the process the magnificent Great Hall (see photograph on p. 135) and Arch were demolished in what would later be referred to as an act of official vandalism. It would surely be a different story today.

Aside from the politics of the time, the new Euston could at last hold its head high, its former reputation of being worse than the old Waterloo gone forever – it had taken more than 60 years for such a statement to be rectified as the rebuilding of Waterloo had commenced soon after the turn of the century. One shudders to think what the situation might have been had the L & B and GWR agreed terms for joint use of the station from 1838 onwards!

Majestic steam on the LMR, 'Duchess' Pacific, No. 46222 *Queen Mary* at the head of the 'Royal Scot'.

Roger Sherlock

Harrow & Wealdstone station on the LNWR line out of Euston. In this period view all is peaceful with two road motors posed on the forecourt. Some years later in the autumn of 1952 the tranquility of the scene was shattered as this was the location of the most devastating accident yet to occur on BR which resulted in the deaths of no less than 122 persons.

Lens of Sutton

North from Euston the main line commenced a steep climb of 1 in 77 (or a rise of 68½ ft. in just one mile). This was the famous Camden bank, the cause of much effort for so many steam expresses starting cold from Euston. It is small wonder that in the earliest days, from 1837 to 1844, the engineers had used cable haulage for trains on Camden bank as it was considered that the steam engines of the time were incapable of hauling trains up such an incline.

Following Camden is the passage through the Hampstead Ridge – then the stations at Hatch End and Watford, both locations which owe much of their early development to the coming of the railway. Another place to change as a direct result of the railway was Willesden. Despite diminishing in size since steam days it is still a massive complex of yards and depôts; yet its origins lie in a small wayside station called Acton Green.

Part of this growth manifested itself as increased suburban traffic in and out of Euston, so that first slow and then relief lines were added parallel to the original route. Work on these commenced in 1875. It was at Willesden that connections were made with the important West London line which itself joined the Southern, Western and Midland systems, and it still carries vast amounts of traffic even today.

A little to the east of Euston was the terminus of the Midland main line at St Pancras. This was another imposing Victorian monolith consisting of seven passenger platforms covered by a single elliptical span roof, 240ft. wide 100ft. high, using no less than 25,000sq.ft. of glass. Trains departed from here for Leicester, Derby and Sheffield from what is still known as the Midland route today. Between 1870 and 1923 it was also used by a number of Great Eastern Railway services operating to Cambridge. Near to the station was a sizeable goods depôt as well as carriage and locomotive servicing facilities.

Broad Street has been mentioned a little earlier it being the terminal for services on the North London Railway system. (Later absorbed into the LNWR). Its history may be

Willesden, 1953; at this time the scene had remained unchanged for over fifty years.

'R.A.' Collection

simplified as a need to provide a service which terminated nearer to the actual City of London – compared with the other stations around the periphery. The LNWR were firm backers of the North London company in promoting this extension. With regard to passenger numbers it was without doubt a popular move, but the same could not be said of approximately 4,500 people whose houses were compulsorily purchased and demolished to facilitate the building of the new railway. It is a little known fact of the period that no alternative accommodation for these wretched individuals was found for this was some years before the Act of 1874 when railway companies were compelled to behave in a more compassionate manner. In spite of the scale of demolition, the actual Broad Street station was very cramped, so much so that the adjacent goods depôt had to be built on two levels.

Passenger traffic to Broad Street was such a success that receipts doubled soon after its opening in 1860. They were to reach a reputed 14 million passenger journeys annually by 1866 which increased still further to 48 million in 1900. It is not surprising that the line was quadrupled as early as 1874.

But the very success of Broad Street was in a way to be its downfall. For being sited so close to the City and operating primarily local trains it was easy prey to competition from the trams and underground system. Consequently from its peak year of 1900, receipts fell as quickly as they had risen and by 1920 had dropped back to 15 million. It would be interesting to know the comparative number of journeys made since that time, although regretfully such figures do not appear to be available.

Despite being involved at the outset, the LNWR seemingly failed to capitalise upon the potential of Broad Street Station. For apart from a London to Wolverhampton service that operated briefly between 1910 and 1915 which originated from the terminus, there was little use made of the facilities it could offer. It remains today a much forgotten

132

station, perhaps the LMR's own equivalent to Marylebone.

East of London the LMS operated a service to Tilbury, Southend and Shoeburyness. During steam days this commenced from St Pancras, but following electrification of the route the London departure station was changed to Fenchurch Street (see Eastern Region notes) in company with the electric services over parts of the former Great Eastern system.

The lines to Southend and Shoeburyness are an example of how, with the passage of time, the commuter has ventured further away from the capital into what was formally argicultural land, even if today it is perhaps hard to imagine certain parts of Essex as anything like open fields. The time scale involved with this change can be gauged by the number of journeys made, although as might be expected it was a gradual rise to start with but gathering momentum all the time. Thus from a figure of 1 million journeys over the LTS route in 1855 there was an increase to 3 million by 1880. But it was from this time on that changes really began to occur and by 1910 no less than 40 million passenger journeys annually were recorded.

Unlike the Southern Region where all the various terminals could really be said to be equal in stature to each other, the charisma of Euston has for years been head and shoulders above that of St Pancras. Perhaps this may have something to do with physical size, for it must be admitted than even the rebuilt Euston is considerably larger than its older neighbour.

It was at both these stations that the products of those great steam engineers, Fowler, Stanier and Ivatt were seen. Who for example could forget the sight of a 'Duchess' Pacific at the head of 15 or 16 coaches on an express for the north? Just north of the terminals in the yards at Willesden or Cricklewood grimy 2-8-0s would arrive and depart at the head of long freight trains, whilst the ring and crash of buffers was a sound occupying the whole of each 24 hours.

A generation later many have forgotten, or perhaps never even heard or seen, such sights and sounds, for instead it is the flash of the overhead electrics from Euston or the high-pitched whistle of the HST sets from St Pancras that dominate the scene. But as with the other routes out of London if you know where to look there are still reminders of a former age. Perhaps a milepost or a notice and certainly several of the buildings themselves. Steam on the LMR may be no more, but in the memory it continues to live on.

LMS THE NIGHT MAIL
THE ENGINEMEN
BY SIR WILLIAM ORPEN, R.A.

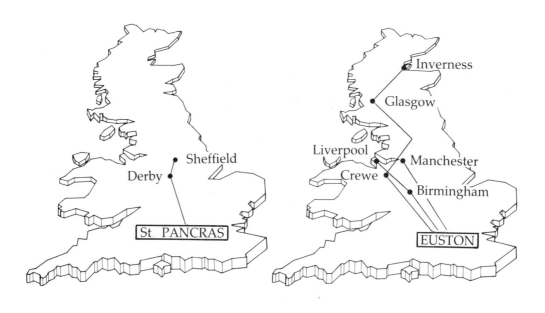

Having referred to the great hall during the Introduction what better than to start with a view inside its cavernous interior. This was built between 1846–9 at what was then an incredible cost of £150,000. Unfortunately its siting effectively split the station in two as a result of successive extensions. This was one of the main waiting areas of the old Euston, shown here during a relatively quiet period. In the distance the stairs led up to the board room. It was in this area that the railway band would congregate at Christmas with the conductor leading the musicians and choir through a rendering of various seasonal carols.

'R.A.' Collection

The approach to Euston station on a gloomy afternoon in 1956, showing that traffic congestion was present even 30 odd years ago. The pórtico and great hall are reached through the archway and it is just possible to glimpse three of the supporting columns of the portico.

'R.A.' Collection

No. 46101 *Royal Scots Grey* at the terminus probably during the late 1950s. The engine carries a '1B' Camden shed plate and is in a rather grimy condition – unfortunately typical for the period when despite jobs being available few youths were prepared to put up with the low wages and deplorable working conditions of the steam age.

Roger Sherlock

Aside from steam it is important not to forget the fourth rail electric service that operated out of Euston to Watford. One of the 3-car M.S.J.A. units can be seen here, with the driving trailer second from the camera. These 3-car units could accommodate 288 2nd-class passengers seated in compartment style carriages – albeit a bit cramped. The view is particularly dated by the oil lamp on the rear of the coach, especially as electric power was readily available.

'R.A.' Collection

Back to steam and this time one of the impressive 'Princess Royal' class of Pacifics, No. 46200 *The Princess Royal* herself. The train is standing at platform 1 following its arrival from Liverpool. Alongside is one of the original LMS diesel-electric locomotives of 1947.

Author Collection

Behind the scenes at Euston and the announcer caught in full voice. Unfortunately, the cavernous interior of most railway stations, coupled with the amount of inherent background noise tended to distort such announcements which for the most part were unintelligible. Besides notifying passengers of arrivals and departures the announcer would also relay special messages, perhaps a lost child or late train arrival and it is for this reason that he is also provided with a number of telephone lines.

'R.A.' Collection

Another look at the behind the scenes activities of a busy station and this time the girl selling refreshments on the platform – nowadays we passengers have to queue. I would think it was most likely that the actual photograph was posed for a publicity shot as the variety of goods on sale is somewhat unusual, even including bottles of wine.

'R.A.' Collection

Another 'Royal Scot', this time No. 46154 *The Hussar* arriving with the 'Ulster Express' and watched by a youthful enthusiast. There were 71 members of the 'Royal Scot' class introduced from 1927 onwards, all were later rebuilt by Sir William Stanier with a taper boiler as seen here.

Author Collection

Departure time, and a spirited get away by a 'Jubilee' at the head of the 'Empress Voyager' express to Liverpool on 11.8.53. Despite the sun shining on the train as it leaves, the interior of the station can be clearly seen as smoky and dingy. Note also the wooden slatted platform.

'R.A.' Collection

No. 46132 *The Kings Regiment Liverpool* just setting off at the head of the 'Irish Mail' express. This particular engine was then allocated to Holyhead depôt, '6J' and so is on a working that will take it back towards its parent shed.

'R.A.' Collection

The temptation when portraying the LMR must be to fill the pages with views of the 'Duchess' Pacifics, after all they were magnificent machines and far more powerful than the first diesels sent to replace them. This is No. 46245 *City of London*, resplendent in maroon livery and no doubt fresh from overhaul. I particularly like the way the crew of the Fowler tank engine behind are casting admiring glances towards the big Pacific, especially as their engine appears somewhat travel-stained.

'R.A.' Collection

To celebrate the coronation of Her Majesty Queen Elizabeth II in 1953, a number of engines ran for a short while with a suitable decoration affixed to the smokebox. Surprisingly few photographs appear to have been taken of the embellishment, shown here attached to No. 46245 *City of London* at Camden depôt on 13.5.53.

'R.A.' Collection

On the former LNWR main line from Euston there were two large locomotive depôts both within a short distance, at Camden and Willesden. Most of the passenger workings were concentrated at the former, whilst Willesden dealt principally with freight locomotives and the various shunting machines for the nearby yards. Naturally, however, there were exceptions, as can be seen in certain of the subsequent photographs. Here though is a normal view, a delightful study of No. 46163 *Civil Service Rifleman* at Camden shed before being made ready for its next duty. In the background is a 'Black 5', No. 44752, one of a number of the class which were modified with roller bearings and caprotti valve gear. 27.6.58.

British Railways

For a short while in the 1950s, BR returned to the pre-war practice of allocating regular crews to particular engines. The intention was to try and ensure that the machines were better looked after and indeed it certainly worked. Unfortunately, the common user policy of later years – brought about by a desire to extract maximum usage from each machine – meant an end to such ideals although for the short while it lasted engines were far cleaner than they had been for a long while. Posed here is Driver W.T. Starvis of Camden in the cab of his allocated engine, No. 46245 *City of London*.

'R.A.' Collection

143

A sad sight, No. 46240 *City of Coventry* in store at Camden 24.3.63. Such was the onset of dieselisation that many engines with years of serviceable life left in them were turned aside in favour of the newer and more modern forms of motive power. Steam development though was far from over, as witness the work of André Chapelon in France. The presence of the sheet over the chimney of No. 46240 meant she would probably never work again.

Roger Sherlock

A 'Jinty', 0-6-0, No. 47675 at Willesden depôt in 1954. These powerful little tanks were used for shunting duties within the London area with several employed at the nearby marshalling yards.

W. Gilburt

Most numerous of all the ex-LMS classes of steam engine were the 'Black 5s', with no less than 842 built from 1934 onwards. Their duties took them over most of the lines of the former company as well as several elsewhere. No. 44836 is on home territory at Willesden, with the cleaners evidently having paid some attention to the cab side but little elsewhere. 29.8.54.

W. Gilburt

One of the last classes to be introduced into LMS steam stock were the Ivatt Class '4' tender engines from 1947 onwards. The high running plate and exposed motion were in complete contrast to the accepted practice of just a few years previously; now the emphasis was on simplicity and ease of access for maintainance. No. 43049 incorporates many features that would later be included on the BR range of standard steam types and is shown here at Willesden in July 1959 in shocking external condition.

M.N.L.P.S.

By the late 1950s the surviving parallel boiler 'Patriot' 4-6-0s were mainly employed on lesser duties, most of the class being rebuilt with a larger capacity taper boiler and enlarged cylinders to increase their power output. No. 45547 was one of 15 members of the original 52 strong class that did not carry names and is seen here outside Willesden shed in 1958. The engine is also coupled to a small Midland-type tender.

Roger Sherlock

Only two members of the 'Jubilee' class carried smoke deflectors, both having been rebuilt in 1942 with a larger boiler and cylinders. No. 45735 and No. 45736 were the engines involved, the latter, perhaps appropriately named *Phoenix* seen at Willesden on 21.10.63.

Roger Sherlock

A 'Jubilee' in more conventional form, No. 45671 *Prince Rupert* between duties at Willesden in August 1962. These engines were similar in appearance to the 'Black 5s' and from a distance it was often difficult to tell the two types apart. When running however the 'Jubilee' produced a more rapid note from the exhaust which was due to the use of three cylinders compared with the 'Black 5s' two.

Roger Sherlock

The ultimate variant of a 'Duchess', No. 46256, named *Sir William Stanier F.R.S.* (after the designer), at Willesden on 10.8.64. This and its sister engine No. 46257, incorporated a number of detail differences compared with the original 'Duchess', which made the pair without doubt the most advanced express steam engine design to successfully work on BR. Unfortunately when the photograph was taken their days were already numbered as witness the yellow stripe on the cabside which indicated that the engine was not to work under the new overhead wires on the main line south of Crewe. As the photograph was taken at Willesden it is interesting to speculate how she arrived in London. Sadly neither No. 46256 nor her sister survived to preservation.

Roger Sherlock

From the sublime to the ridiculous, with No. 47340 shunting a D.M.U. driving trailer at Willesden in 1963. The chalked inscription on the bunker side reads '2 gulp' and must have meant something to someone.

Roger Sherlock

An often forgotten side of railway operation was that of maintainance to the
infrastructure – how many views are seen
of signals being cleaned? Here two
workers are engaged on cleaning and
lubricating a gantry of three LNWR arms
on Camden bank in 1953, now long since
replaced by colour lights.

'R.A.' Collection

Empty stock working out of Euston towards the carriage sidings at Willesden with Class 4, 2-6-4T,
No. 80067 in charge. The steepness of the gradient is apparent from the background of the
photograph and was one of the reasons why such stock movements were usually entrusted to
machines like the large Class 4 tanks.

'R.A.' Collection

Another empty stock working, this time with a Stanier design tank. Comparing this with the previous view it is perhaps easy to see how the BR standard design was derived from the earlier LMS-type.

Roger Sherlock

A 'Britannia' this time, No. 70033 *Charles Dickens* on the rise of Camden bank with a down express in September 1953. On the right-hand side are the relief lines, while in the centre the cables and troughing are connected with the fourth rail electrification which it is just possible to discern on the extreme left.

'R.A.' Collection

Seen from a passing train No. 45736 *Samson* is nearing the end of its journey to Euston in July 1959, the fireman evidently glad to take a breather with his work completed.

Eric Best

No. 46135 *The East Lancashire Regiment* working hard near the top of Camden bank at the head of a heavy train of ex-LMS stock. In the background colour light signals have replaced the semaphore arms, although it is just possible to make out what appears to be a very old mechanical ground signal to the right of the first coach.

M.N.L.P.S.

No. 45531 *Sir Frederick Harrison* sweeps majestically along at Camden at the head of its train, the front vehicle of which is a former GWR siphon milk van. The electrified lines are on the right this time, with the four rail system – 2 running rails and two electric rails, easily identified.

'R.A.' Collection

152

Double-heading was a relatively frequent, if enormously uneconomic, method of working during steam days. Here an unidentified pairing of a 'Patriot' and 'Royal Scot' are working hard at Camden bank during 1953. The use of two engines on one train could be for several reasons, but was usually because the load was above the limit set down for the train engine itself.

'R.A.' Collection

For a short time following nationalisation, BR experimented with a number of liveries and variations in ownership insignia. One of these is shown here on No. 46241 *City of Edinburgh*, seen at Kensal Green on an express working, carrying dark blue paintwork and with 'British Railways' in full on the tender. The engine is also interesting in that the top of the smokebox can be seen to slope down, indicating that this particular engine had previously been streamlined. Smokeboxes of this type were later altered to the more conventional cylindrical pattern.

Author Collection

Part of the vast expanse of Willesden yard photographed on 1.1.54. The site here occupied a vast acreage and included facilities for goods and passenger vehicle storage as well as the locomotive shed seen earlier. Most obvious from the photograph are the number of small capacity wagons of varying types, including a small container vehicle. Notice also the 'Royal Mail' coach partly obscured by the overhead gantry.

'R.A.' Collection

Shunting in Willesden yard on a foggy day in early 1954. Just visible in the distance are the actual sorting sidings with the shunter calling the train back into the appropriate road. Such a procedure was both time consuming and labour intensive especially when small wagons were involved. Although it has contracted greatly, Willesden is today still one of the largest remaining yards on BR and handles a considerable amount of traffic in any 24-hour period.

'R.A.' Collection

A rebuilt 'Patriot', No. 45523 *Bangor* alongside the platform at Willesden Junction in 1958. An interesting comparison is available when comparing this engine with one in original condition – see p. 146. The rebuilt engines greatly resembled the 'Royal Scot' class even if the 'Patriots' were somewhat less powerful.

Roger Sherlock

Working out its last days before withdrawal, No. 46144 *Honourable Artillery Company* is at the head of a mixed freight near Willesden in September 1963. The engine is in shocking external condition and yet appears mechanically sound if the lack of obvious steam leaks and blowing off from the safety valves is anything to go by. Notice the modern flat-bottom rail although only of short lengths compared with that used today.

Roger Sherlock

A steam suburban service, believed to be near Bushey. No. 80064 is at the head of seven vehicles of varying vintage, the first coach of which has a side observation window for the guard, once a commonplace feature. Notice also the small 'SC' plate beneath the allocation, indicating that the engine is fitted with a self-cleaning smokebox.

W. Gilburt

No. 48074 to Stanier's basic design for heavy freight, the 2-8-0 on the duty for which it was intended near Watford. Over 600 of these engines were built from 1935 onwards, with a number venturing overseas during the war years, some as far as the Middle East and Eastern Europe.

'R.A.' Collection

No. 45109 and an unknown 'Princess' on the 'Merseyside Express' near Watford. The family similarity between a number of Stanier's designs is obvious, in many ways akin to that of the various Great Western classes – no wonder perhaps when it is known that the designer spent several years working at Swindon.

'R.A.' Collection

Another Class 5, this time No. 45276 on empty stock. Underneath all that grime the engine was carrying a smart black livery, shortage of labour for cleaning on BR meant such an appearance was all too commonplace.

'R.A.' Collection

At the head of some 12 vehicles weighing perhaps in excess of 400 tons gross, No. 46168 *The Girl Guide* is making good progress near Watford on 21.8.57.

'R.A.' Collection

The advantage of the 'Jubilee' class was their versatility when it came to the types of train they could handle, anything from a heavy freight to all but the fastest express. Here No. 45653 *Barham* is in charge of a top link working – Willesden duty W243, even if the shed plate shows the engine allocated to Blackpool!

'R.A.' Collection

Seen from a low angle the sheer size of the 'Princess Royal' Pacifics is revealed and here No. 46201 *Princess Elizabeth* is at the head of the 'Mid-Day Scot' express. There were 13 members in the class, one of Sir William Stanier's first designs for the LMS from which the larger 'Duchess' class engines were derived.

'R.A.' Collection

Another impressive low angle shot, this time showing No. 45534 *E. Tootal Broadhurst* to advantage at the head of a down express. This was one of the 'Patriot' class of engines rebuilt in BR days, the protrusion just behind the vacuum pipe being the cover at the end of the inside cylinder.

'R.A.' Collection

Away from the express services for a moment and another '8F', this time No. 48304 at the head of an up freight possibly bound for Willesden. Together with the ex-Midland route, the former LNWR main line carried a considerable amount of freight. In steam days much of this was coal which was intended for both industrial and private use.

'R.A.' Collection

Fourteen in tow for No. 46225, *Duchess of Gloucester* on the down 'Mid-Day Scot' near Berkhamsted in June 1953. The variety of coaches is particularly interesting and yet this was not unusual at the time. Also noteworthy was the then standard practice of adding extra vehicles should the loading necessitate it. The only limitation was a practical one in that such trains had to be accommodated at the various station platforms en route.

'R.A.' Collection

A rebuilt 'Patriot' 4-6-0, No. 45530 *Sir Frank Ree* near Watford on an up express. Just visible in the smoke deflectors are a pair of hand holes which were cut into the sheets to avoid having a handrail which might obstruct further the already restricted forward view so typical of the steam engine.

'R.A.' Collection

Moving away from the Birmingham route to St Pancras, the London terminus of the former Midland main line. No. 40029 waiting to depart on an empty stock working. The large pipe running from the smokebox to the side tank indicates the engine is one of 20 members of the class which were equipped for condensing and so able to work through the tunnels to Moorgate. Theoretically this fitting enabled the engine to consume its own exhaust steam, although in practice it tended to raise the temperature of the water so much that the injectors would not work correctly, thus drivers would avoid its use whenever possible.

Roger Sherlock

Ivatt Class '4', No. 43019 waiting to leave the terminus on a 'Swedish Lloyd' line boat train to Tilbury, 21.10.61. Just before the photograph had been taken the fireman had gone to some trouble in carefully chalking up the headcode, although to little avail as it should have read 'IE05'!

M. Mensing

St Pancras was resignalled by BR around 1957, with a new colour light gantry soon to replace the semaphore bracket. Just entering the terminus is No. 10201, one of the SR main line diesels at the time working on the Midland main line to Derby. Along with their sisters, the LMS diesels, these engines were very much the forerunners of the first generation of main line diesels used by BR from 1958 onwards.

Author Collection

To cater for steam engines working freight on the Midland line towards London there was a depôt at Cricklewood. Also sited here was a sizeable marshalling yard, as well as other yards nearby, together with a milk factory. '8F', No. 48206 seen in relatively clean condition and coupled to a grimy sister engine outside the steam shed in the early 1950s.

W. Gilburt

For many years the Midland Railway had operated a small engine policy, preferring to double-head trains when necessary rather than build bigger machines. No. 43565 is an example of that policy, dating back to 1885 and for some 20 years the standard goods engine of the MR. She is shown at Cricklewood depôt.

W. Gilburt

In comparison with the previous view here is one of the BR Standard designs, clearly showing how steam had developed over the years to 1953 when the first of the Class 4, 76xxx engines were introduced. No. 76088 was a Cricklewood based engine and a number of other engines of the class were allocated to the Southern Region.

M.N.L.P.S.

A sight now long gone from BR is that of the cattle train; despite making one wonder about the economics of needing approximately 25 lorries to replace just one train. Double-chimneyed 2-6-0, No. 43039 in charge of a livestock working near Elstree in August 1953.

'R.A.' Collection

Such was the shortage of suitable wagons on this particular day that a number of containers have been placed in open wagons. No. 44858 at the head of a mixed freight just after leaving Elstree tunnel in 1953.

'R.A.' Collection

An unusual pairing of a '4F', No. 44043 and a BR 'Class 4' tank near Elstree on a local passenger working. The '4F' class were an obvious development from the smaller '3F' type depicted earlier, although, even then they were woefully inadequate for many of the trains then running. These engines also had a reputation for rough riding.

'R.A.' Collection

A delightful study of No. 45626 *Seychelles* framed in the tunnel mouth at Elstree in the summer of 1953. On the right is a permanent way hut used by the local gang engaged in track maintainance. During the summer months most of their time would be spent on grass cutting which was intended to reduce the fire risk at the lineside.

'R.A.' Collection

Emerging from the gloom of the tunnel, No. 42300 is working hard near Elstree in 1953. This particular tank engine was one of 125 built from 1927 onwards and intended for suburban traffic. Withdrawals amongst the class commenced early in the BR modernisation plan and by 1962 half, including No. 42300, had already been consigned for scrap. The remainder followed soon after.

'R.A.' Collection

Another pairing and this time one of the Midland 4-4-0s, No. 40542 attached to a 'Black 5'. The 4-4-0 design were the main type of passenger engine used on the MR; there were several varieties including a number of compounds.

'R.A.' Collection

The massive exterior of the former North London Railway terminus at Broad Street from which connections were available to east and west London.

Lens of Sutton

Memories of years long past, as a former North London Railway 0-6-0 tank sets off from Broad Street on an LCGB special working. Fourteen engines of this type survived into BR ownership and one passed into preservation. It is currently on the Bluebell Railway in Sussex.

Lens of Sutton

Modernisation of sorts at Poplar Docks in July 1953. The photograph shows one of the new 4-ton containers intended for a variety of traffic and seen here discharging its load of stone into a waiting lorry. This particular idea did not catch on.

'R.A.' Collection

Last rites for steam at Shoeburyness on the LTS line, 27.2.63. A 3-cylinder Stanier 2-6-4, No. 42501 has arrived at the station and is in the process of running round prior to returning to St. Pancras. To witness the occasion a group of men from the former steam shed are posed alongside the engine, the shed of course closing in consequence of the electrification. Notice the white buffers of the tank engine as well as its clean condition – no doubt specially prepared for the day. Unfortunately removal of the grime has revealed a number of scratches to the bunker side.

'R.A.' Collection